When God Speaks

Exploring the Absurd and Outrageous Commands of
God

Tom Kinnan

Sermon To Book
www.sermontobook.com

When God Speaks / Tom Kinnan
ISBN-13: 978-1-945793-48-6
ISBN-10: 1-945793-48-1

No one has impacted my preaching or presentations more than my love, my partner in life. Her name is Kathy, but I call her Queenie.

Many thought it was absurd that she married me. She has read every sermon I have ever preached before I presented it and critiqued it. Outrageous I know. And yeah … it has created more than one "discussion." But she has been a refining fire for me.

This book is dedicated to Queenie, her abiding love, and her investment in me. I love her.

CONTENTS

By Faith…

Now faith is confidence in what we hope for and assurance about what we do not see. This is what the ancients were commended for. By faith we understand that the universe was formed at God's command, so that what is seen was not made out of what was visible.

—Hebrews 11:1–3

I read the story of a fourth-grader named Patrick who decided he would take his Legos to school. His favorite Lego piece was a little policeman figure—seemingly harmless, right?

But when Patrick placed a two-inch plastic gun in the policeman's hand, the nine-year-old discovered what "zero tolerance" really meant. The school flipped out. They determined that the miniature plastic "gun" was a weapon, and Patrick was temporarily suspended from school.[1]

Now, we all know that Legos are pretty lethal weapons. If you've ever stepped on one, then you've experienced just how much damage they can do. But would you categorize a two-inch plastic Lego gun as a threat big enough to nearly expel a fourth grader?

Things such as this leave me flabbergasted. The absurdity and lack of reason is so confusing that I walk away, saying, "I just don't get it."

Many people have that same attitude about their faith. They look at the Bible, Jesus, and Christians and they say, "I don't get it." They think they can't be like Jesus or don't possess enough faith to move forward in any kind of religious expression. Or, they think faith is simply a crutch people conjure up to help them deal with life, believing faith has no bearing on reality.

It can be easy for us as Christians to dismiss the above statements. In fact, it's *easier* for us not to deal with them. But I believe we need to face them head on. We need to address criticisms of our faith—not run from them.

So, let's begin a journey. In this book we'll look at some of the most absurd, outrageous commands God gave His people in the Bible. We'll unpack what happened, why it mattered, and how we can learn from those situations. After each chapter, application-focused workbook sections will help you discover how these extreme commands are relevant to your life today. I hope our faith is rattled and challenged. And I hope we will make up our minds to say "yes" to even the absurd, outrageous commands of God.

What do *absurd* and *outrageous* mean? *Absurd* means

something that is ridiculously incongruous or unreasonable. And outrageous means something that is unconventional, something that pushes the boundaries beyond what is expected.

So, when we say we're dealing with the absurd, outrageous commands of God, we're dealing with things that seem unreasonable and far outside the bounds of what we would consider sane or usual.

We may struggle to see how these commands can be a benefit to us. We may struggle to see how they fit and work in our lives every single day. We may be tempted to say, "I don't get it" and walk away.

But God's commands aren't necessarily meant to match our level of understanding. Rather, they are meant to meet our challenges. They help us to move into a whole new world of living by God's grace and power.

It's when we look at the absurd, outrageous commands of God that faith struts its stuff. It's when we recognize that, even though we don't understand it all, we *trust* Him to work for the good. It's then that faith stands up, flexes its muscles, and takes us beyond the realm of the ordinary.

There's nothing ordinary about God. When we understand that, we realize that the absurd and outrageous things in His world are normal. They're expected. They're anticipated. And they're for our good.

One thing about faith, it is not stationary. It always steps off the cliff. It always gets out there. Faith can be unreasonable, unthinkable, unyielding, unbelievable, or unpredictable, but it is not static.

We know by faith that what appears on the surface to be absurd or unreasonable is, in fact, solid and necessary.

By faith we become obedient to what God commands.

In her book *One Thousand Gifts*, Ann Voskamp talks about how faith propels us into the holy and raises us above the ordinary. I love this picture of truth:

> To know God is more than "aching for more than ordinary." On the plane of God and in the dimension of true reality, there is no ordinary. Ordinary ceases to exist. When we are reborn, we're drenched with wonder. The day, me, the world, it drips. To know God is to realize there's no such thing as ordinary and all our ache is only for more of His glory.[2]

In this book, we're going to look at some significant faith stories dealing with absurd, outrageous commands of God. As you pick up this book to read, you have some options. You can become a spectator—an observer of the information offered on the pages to follow. This could become just another notch on your books to read list.

Or, you can decide to engage with the challenges and principles presented in the book.

As we go on this journey together, be thinking about that one thing that you know God is telling you, but that you've brushed aside, chalking it up to being "too absurd," "too outrageous." And then ask God to show you how your faith needs to be adjusted so that you can change your mindset and get on board with the absurd and outrageous.

Don't shy away from God's commands. When you hear Him speak, don't run, fearing you will be in over your head. God's commands may seem absurd and outrageous, but they will keep you safe and make you everlasting.

Prepare to journey on this faith trek. Prepare to have your faith challenged. And prepare to say *"yes!"* to what you think are the absurd, outrageous commands of God.

CHAPTER ONE

Build an Ark!

So make yourself an ark of cypress wood; make rooms in it and coat it with pitch inside and out.
—Genesis 6:14

Have you ever been in a work or life situation in which people start to poke fun at Christianity? They often start by scoffing at some point of morality with which they disagree. And from there, the ridicule moves to making fun of "hypocritical Christians" and "fire and brimstone" church teachings.

If you've never experienced this, then be happy. Be very happy. But if you have experienced it, then you know how intense it can get.

Today, people question God's power and presence. They mock Him. They use God's name as an expletive or punctuation mark and seldom acknowledge who He is. I'm amazed whenever I hear God's name used as an exclamation point. But many of us say it all the time without even giving it a thought.

While it's easy to think of this behavior as something only for unbelievers, the truth is that even Christians live as close to the edge as possible. We claim Him in name but not in practice.

We filter life through our opinions and a secular worldview, rather than through His Word and a Christ-centered worldview. We tend to determine our worldview based on news and media, the opinions of others, experience, or secular education. We're not even sure how to think with a Christian mindset and weigh things according to what God wants anymore.

Society's norms do not reflect God's norms. Our society has rejected truth. We set our course based on our human desires, which come with fences, boundaries, and sometimes fear of extending beyond our areas of comfort.

That's why, when God calls us to do something, we need to take heed. We need to realize that He sees something in us—a glimmer of hope, a measure of righteousness. And despite our fallen ways, we need to respond.

We need to understand that, if God calls us to go somewhere, talk to somebody, do something, or give something we think is outside the bounds of reason, He must have confidence in who we are. He doesn't ask us to do what can't be done if it can't be done!

And if we are obedient, the unreasonable can actually occur.

Noah was not saved by his skills—he wasn't a fisherman or a carpenter or an engineer. Noah was saved by his character, heart, and obedience. And it's an incredible lesson for us as we think about the things that God is calling us to do for Him.

Obedience over Understanding

This is the account of Noah and his family. Noah was a righteous man, blameless among the people of his time, and he walked faithfully with God. Noah had three sons: Shem, Ham and Japheth.

Now the earth was corrupt in God's sight and was full of violence. God saw how corrupt the earth had become, for all the people on earth had corrupted their ways. So God said to Noah, "I am going to put an end to all people, for the earth is filled with violence because of them. I am surely going to destroy both them and the earth. So make yourself an ark of cypress wood; make rooms in it and coat it with pitch inside and out. This is how you are to build it: The ark is to be three hundred cubits long, fifty cubits wide and thirty cubits high. Make a roof for it, leaving below the roof an opening one cubit high all around. Put a door in the side of the ark and make lower, middle and upper decks. I am going to bring floodwaters on the earth to destroy all life under the heavens, every creature that has the breath of life in it. Everything on earth will perish. But I will establish my covenant with you, and you will enter the ark—you and your sons and your wife and your sons' wives with you. You are to bring into the ark two of all living creatures, male and female, to keep them alive with you. Two of every kind of bird, of every kind of animal and of every kind of creature that moves along the ground will come to you to be kept alive. You are to take every kind of food that is to be eaten and store it away as food for you and for them."

Noah did everything just as God commanded him.
—Genesis 6:9–22

At the time Noah built his ark, he hadn't experienced

rain as we do. Rather, every morning, a mist arose from the ground and watered the earth (Genesis 2:6). So, when God told Noah to build an ark and prepare for a massive flood, we could call that an absurd, outrageous command of God!

But I remind you—God's commands aren't necessarily meant to match your understanding; they are meant to meet your challenges.

Look at this situation. God told Noah to build an ark. Noah had to have been confused! He wasn't a fisherman. He didn't use boats. How would he even know what an ark was? The concept of a flood was so absurd and outrageous that Noah's understanding of the command could have begun to sink right out of the dock. But, in spite of having seen no rainfall, he did see the need to obey.

And not only was Noah expected to build an ark for something called a "flood," but he also had to store food away for his family and all the animals. I can't even imagine the overwhelming challenge of this task! A floating zoo complete with a cafeteria for all the animals and people.

Some of us have trouble putting together menus for our families, let alone taking care of all the animals in the world. And most people don't know what different kinds of food animals eat, or where to get that food. Noah had to face all of this, and he had to get it right.

If that wasn't enough, if you go to Hebrews chapter 11, which is known as the faith chapter, it gives us a little more insight into the situation and Noah's faith. Just by building the ark, Noah was condemning the people around him. The boat was a physical representation of God's judgment that was about to fall. So, there he was, condemning those around him, while also looking like an idiot. To any bystander, Noah's actions would have made no sense at all.

It's no doubt that this was an absurd, outrageous command.

A Point of No Return

When God flooded the earth, humanity was violent and corrupt. We were godless beyond imagination, and the God we denied and ignored had had enough.

It's hard to imagine driving God to a breaking point, but perhaps that's not the best way to look at this.

Sin and God do not coexist over the long haul. Yes, He is patient and continues to pursue us even when we turn our backs on Him, but in the case of Noah's time, humanity had become irrevocably unrepentant.

God saw what had happened, and He was not about to allow humanity to progress as a totally degenerate population. So, instead, He opted to destroy humanity and the earth. It was time for a "do over."

The LORD saw how great the wickedness of the human race had become on the earth, and that every inclination of the thoughts of the human heart was only evil all the time. The LORD regretted that he had made human beings on the earth, and his heart was deeply troubled. So the LORD said, "I will wipe from the face of the earth the human race I have created—and with them the animals, the birds and the creatures that move along the ground—for I regret that I have made them."

—Genesis 6:5–7

Humanity takes life to corrupt levels, but God raises life to holy levels.

We take that which is holy and make it unholy. We attack and malign; we ignore and neglect; we corrupt and disdain what God says and does. Our arrogance makes us think that since God's directives are not obvious, or comfortable, or convenient, or politically correct, they must be wrong.

But either God is the beginning and the end (Revelation 22:13), or He isn't. Either He determines what is corrupt, or He doesn't. Our opinion, our preference, our desire is not the determining factor. Our thoughts will never trump God's (Isaiah 55:8–9). Our books will never negate His. Our accusations and sentencing of God's desires will never imprison the power or plan of God. He determines what is corrupt. His Word stands (Psalm 119:89). So, when God says enough is enough, then that's that. Enough is enough!

Another reality we can't ignore that seems a bit ominous is that it's possible to reach a point of no return. I know it sounds scary, but it's true, and there are two ways that we will run into this "point of no return" with God.

The first happens the moment we die. In that moment, there is no possibility of altering the plan we have put into motion. There is no "do over." If, in my lifetime, I refused to surrender my life to Christ, if I refused to live with Him, if I said there is no God, there is no hell, and if I denied all the realities of the Scriptures, then my death would be a point of no return. It'd be too late to change my mind and my heart.

Another point of no return is when God has had

enough. When this happens, He will act, and He will do what He sees fit to put things right. Two examples of this stick out to me. The first took place when God destroyed humanity with a flood. The other occurred in the story of Ananias and Sapphira in Acts 5:1–11.

At the time Ananias and Sapphira lived, the church functioned by people selling everything they had and living together as a community (Acts 4:32–35). They cared for one another and relied on one another, but it wasn't by law, edict, or anything God had predetermined. It was just how the church had been functioning.

So, in Acts we learn of the story of Ananias and Sapphira. They stood before Peter and said, "Hey, we sold our land, everything we have, and we've come to give the proceeds to you."

Peter asked them if it was truly everything, and they said "yes." It was all they had received for the land.

But they were lying. They were holding back. And it was because of this lie that Ananias and Sapphira were struck dead on the spot.

I've often thought, *Man, God, look at David.* I mean, David was a murderer and an adulterer (2 Samuel 11:1–24). He did a lot of stuff that we would find to be nearly unforgiveable. Yet Scripture calls him "the beloved of God." And then we have Ananias and Sapphira, who told one lie and were immediately struck dead. *What?* That doesn't seem fair!

It's easy to simply brush the real issue aside and say that God is unpredictable and unfair, but then we're missing the point. God knows the heart. He knows when we're sincere, and He knows when we're insincere.

So, this point of no return has to do with a sincere sickness of the heart. A sincere rejection of God. A sincere lack of heartfelt belief.

It begs the question: Are we genuinely open to the Lord and sincere? Are we listening to what He has to say? Are we willing to build an ark? Are we willing to obey His absurd, outrageous commands?

Noah was.

God Qualifies the Righteous

If we go back to the Genesis passage that introduces Noah, notice that it doesn't start with sin. Yes, the verses leading into the passage talk about the horrible state of the world, but when Noah shows up, the tone is much different.

> *But Noah found favor in the eyes of the LORD. This is the account of Noah and his family. Noah was a righteous man, blameless among the people of his time, and he walked faithfully with God.*
>
> *—Genesis 6:8–9*

Yes, the world had been overrun by sin. But righteousness still reigned because God reigned. And whenever God is involved, He always starts with that which is righteous and holy.

The task set before Noah must have consumed his life. Not only was he building this incredible ark, but he had a family for which to care. He needed to provide for them and meet their needs—all while rounding up animals and planning for a big voyage into who knows where.

But if we look closely, we see that Noah had two qualifications for building the ark. First, the Bible says that he was righteous (Genesis 6:9), and second, it says that Noah had a "holy fear" of God (Hebrews 11:7).

A holy fear means that he was reverent. He had a deep respect and awe for God; he held Him in high esteem.

So, while, on the outside, it might seem as if the task to build an ark while caring for his family and preparing for the coming judgment was a bit out of Noah's league, God knew what was in the heart. He knew Noah to be righteous, and He knew that Noah had a healthy fear of God.

What qualified Noah weren't his skills—it was his character and heart. Don't think that your skill set, gifts, or what you have qualifies you to answer God's call. God chooses His servants based on who we are, not what we do. It's not only our gifts; it's not only our skills. It's not that I want to earn brownie points; it's not that I'm somehow assuring myself of a better spot in the presence of God. God chooses us for who we are, and He takes us beyond who we think we can be and raises us to a higher level.

Sometimes we think we live in a world where everything around us is going south. There's so much sin and corruption. It's easy to wonder whether God even notices anything good that happens. But the story of Noah proves that He does.

When we serve the Lord, when we open ourselves to Him, when we say "yes" to the absurd, to the outrageous, we stand out, and our "yes" shows a lot about what's in our heart.

Righteous Responsibility Brings Reward

Too often we want God's grace without giving. We want salvation without service. We want it easy.

But God has a place for you—not only in heaven, but also here on earth. He longs to use every one of us in a productive manner, much like He used Noah.

I'm amazed at how often we come into the presence of God and we say, "Lord, forgive me, save me, cleanse me, make everything right, but don't ask anything of me."

It's as if we're telling God that we want the baby without the pain. We want all of the rewards but none of the work. None of the responsibility.

And then there was Noah.

He was bombarded by people telling him he was crazy, telling him he was wasting his time. It's hard to go against the grain, yet Noah stayed true. He got the job done for God.

We cannot live in this world without being affected by it, and I'm certain that Noah felt the pressure from his neighbors' taunts. I'm sure there were many days when Noah got up and thought, "I must be a nutcase. What on earth am I doing?" He was bombarded every day with influences that were counter to God's will.

But God also affirmed Noah daily. God would speak to him and affirm what he was doing. Though he was not unaffected by what was going on around him, he was undeterred. He kept on doing what God had called him to do.

No doubt many of us would have said, "God, why did You ask me to do something that would bring such shame to me and my family?" You know you would have! We often blame God and question His will if we find ourselves in the midst of a struggle.

But God's commands are meant to provide refuge in the midst of storms. When we think that God is asking us to do something that seems insane, if we just push through, we'll discover that it was actually a refuge that protected and cared for us, enabling us to move forward.

God didn't ask Noah to build the ark so that he would be ridiculed. He asked him to build it so he would be saved.

When God calls us, it's easy to think, "He wants something from me. I don't think I want to hang around here." But we'd better hang around.

We may think it's outrageous and absurd, or that God will demand too much. But whatever He is asking of us is necessary. It's necessary for you and for those around you.

You don't need to fear the absurd, outrageous commands of God. You should look for them. They are signals and signs that will save you.

Lord, You know I've been guilty of not doing all that You ask. I've questioned a lot of things, and there are things now that rumble around in my mind that I still don't grasp. But I don't want to get bogged down in that. I don't want to look at what You ask as being absurd and outrageous. I want to trust You.

Remind me that there is nothing ordinary about You and Your plan.

Challenge me. Rattle my cage, so that I stop asking for more, more, more and instead take on the responsibility that comes with answering Your call.

Do Your work, I pray, and I give You the praise. In Christ's name. Amen.

WORKBOOK

Chapter One Questions

Question: What made the building of the ark seem ridiculous to Noah's neighbors? Have you ever been mocked for following God?

_____

_____

_____

_____

_____

_____

_____

_____

_____

_____

_____

Question: What does it mean to be at a point of no return? What is the difference between a Christian and a non-Christian reaching this point?

_____

_____

_____

_____

_____

_____

_____

_____

_____

_____

_____

Question: Describe the time and effort required for Noah to build the ark. What were his qualifications for this enormous task? What is something that God has called you to do that requires a long time and arduous work on your part?

_____

_____

_____

_____

_____

_____

_____

_____

_____

_____

_____

_____

Action: _Righteous responsibility brings reward._ Make a list of some of the rewards with which you wish to see God bless you. Then, next to each, write out your "righteous responsibility" toward making it happen.

_____

_____

_____

_____

_____

_____

_____

_____

_____

_____

_____

Chapter One Notes

_____

_____

_____

_____

_____

_____

_____

_____

_____

_____

_____

_____

_____

_____

_____

_____

_____

_____

_____

_____

_____

_____

_____

CHAPTER TWO

Kill Your Son!

*Some time later God tested Abraham. He said to him,
"Abraham!" "Here I am," he replied. Then God said, "Take
your son, your only son, whom you love—Isaac—and go to
the region of Moriah. Sacrifice him there as a burnt offering on a mountain I will show you."*
—Genesis 22:1–2

Windows allow us to see into buildings and houses.
The dirtier the window, the harder it is to get a good
glimpse of what is inside. But when a window is clean and
the sun hits it just right? Everything is illuminated. Light
streams onto the floor. People and pets alike bask in its
warmth.

Imagine that you're a window. The Lord wants to shine
His glory not only in you, but through you so that as you
interact with others, people see Christ.

We can't turn toward God until we've allowed Christ
to do a spiritual housecleaning in us. Apologizing to people we've hurt is a good piece of that, but it's not the

whole process. We need to clear the air for sure, but we also need to be ready to respond to the light that will be coming in the window from God's Spirit.

As we continue with the absurd, outrageous commands of God, we shouldn't stand back from the light that will come when we do what He's asked us to do.

We must take inventory of our lives—get rid of what is dragging us down, what is fogging up the windows—and become obedient to God. Why? Because we want our desires to match His desires.

Sometimes I think we ask the wrong question when taking an inventory of our Christian lives. Typically, we ask, "What does God want me to let go of so I can do the things He has for me?"

But perhaps it would be more incisive or cutting if we asked, "Is there anything I am withholding from God?"

Holding Back

If we say we're really giving our lives over to the Lord, then there's nothing we would withhold from Him. Yet, like Ananias and Sapphira, most of us do hold a few things back. We want to live as clean windows, yet we also want our pile of junk over in the corner.

The absurd, outrageous command of God that smacks this issue in the face is when God told Abraham, "Kill your son":

> *Early the next morning Abraham got up and loaded his donkey. He took with him two of his servants and his son*

Isaac. When he had cut enough wood for the burnt offering, he set out for the place God had told him about. On the third day Abraham looked up and saw the place in the distance. He said to his servants, "Stay here with the donkey while I and the boy go over there. We will worship and then we will come back to you."

Abraham took the wood for the burnt offering and placed it on his son Isaac, and he himself carried the fire and the knife. As the two of them went on together, Isaac spoke up and said to his father Abraham, "Father?"

"Yes, my son?" Abraham replied.

"The fire and wood are here," Isaac said, "but where is the lamb for the burnt offering?"

Abraham answered, "God himself will provide the lamb for the burnt offering, my son." And the two of them went on together.

When they reached the place God had told him about, Abraham built an altar there and arranged the wood on it. He bound his son Isaac and laid him on the altar, on top of the wood. Then he reached out his hand and took the knife to slay his son. But the angel of the LORD called out to him from heaven, "Abraham! Abraham!"

"Here I am," he replied.

"Do not lay a hand on the boy," he said. "Do not do anything to him. Now I know that you fear God, because you have not withheld from me your son, your only son."

Abraham looked up and there in a thicket he saw a ram caught by its horns. He went over and took the ram and sacrificed it as a burnt offering instead of his son. So Abraham called that place The LORD Will Provide. And to this day it is said, "On the mountain of the LORD it will be provided."

—Genesis 22:3–14

Think about that. Just let it settle in. God asked Abraham to kill his own child. Can you imagine?

Had God given me that command, I think we would've had a conversation. I'd have said, "What are You talking about? Are You not thinking, God? Don't You realize all the promises You've made to me are embodied in my son?"

I think I would have had to duke it out with God.

Abraham didn't take the command lightly—but he also didn't do much to fight it. When God said, "Abraham, I want you to sacrifice your son," Abraham was ready to obey.

The Lord Provides

To get the full impact of how absurd and outrageous this command was, you must understand the context of Abraham's life up to that point.

Abraham and his wife, Sarah, were old and childless, yet God promised them that their descendants would be as numerous as the stars in the sky (Genesis 22:17). He also promised them a land flowing with milk and honey, and He promised that He would never leave them.

Now, Abraham could have easily dismissed these promises. Again, he was old. Sarah seemed to be barren. How could God possibly line all of this up for him? But Abraham didn't question. He acted. He obeyed God, because he believed God.

He headed for Canaan, which would become the Promised Land, and at ninety-nine years old, he became the father of Isaac (Genesis 17:1). It must have seemed as though all of God's promises were coming together.

So, imagine the shock Abraham must have experienced when God commanded him to sacrifice his son! Isaac had been a promise from God! He was the key to everything that the Lord had in store for Abraham and his descendants. And yet the command was clear.

So, instead of arguing or throwing a fit or turning his back on God, Abraham obeyed without any apparent delay.

Abraham and Isaac headed out to Moriah, and I have to wonder what the journey was like. Were they laughing together? Were they having a good time, making good memories? Isaac was probably enjoying the journey, but I'm thinking Abraham was pretty somber.

Finally, three days later, they arrived at their destination. Abraham told the servants who had traveled with them to stay put. He and Isaac grabbed the fire and the wood, and they headed up the mountain to make what Isaac assumed was an animal sacrifice.

As they journeyed, Isaac asked about the lamb. Abraham assured him the Lord would provide the sacrifice.

Sure enough, He did.

Abraham laid Isaac on the wood and pulled out his knife to kill Isaac. As Abraham raised his knife to kill his son, God's angel from heaven shouted: "'Do not lay a hand on the boy,' he said. 'Do not do anything to him. Now I know that you fear God, because you have not withheld from me your son, your only son'" (Genesis 22:12).

Can you imagine the relief Abraham must have felt? He cut his son loose.

Abraham heard the bleat of a ram, and saw the animal caught by its horns in the thicket. Yes, God had provided the sacrifice, indeed.

Abraham named the place where this incident occurred "The Lord Has Provided," because God had been faithful to His promises.

Do You Believe?

Abraham withheld nothing from God, not even his son, the person who represented all of God's promises and blessing. When Abraham's spiritual character was put to the test, he passed with flying colors.

I want you to understand something about Abraham's thought processes: Now, remember that at this point he was still getting acquainted with God. He was still coming to discover God's faithfulness and goodness. So, when God gave a directive that seemed so absurd, it was the ultimate test. And in the end, Abraham learned *even more* of God's love and faithfulness. He came out of that test with an even greater faith level!

I think one reason we struggle with obedience is that we don't always believe God. I can believe God that He'll do things and provide for someone else—that He'll take care of them and answer their prayers. But for me, I'm not always so sure God will come through.

It's always easier to obey, or trust God, for the lives of others than it is for ourselves.

So, it begs the question: Do we really believe God? Do we do what He says because we believe Him? Abraham believed the promises God had made, even to the point that he was ready to sacrifice his very own son.

Do we have that level of faith? Or are we holding on to things, hoping God will shine His light through our window anyway?

Whatever the Request, the Answer Is "Yes!"

Here are some quick lessons we can glean from this chapter:

First, what we sometimes label as being *unthinkable*, an obedient servant would label as being *unquestionable*. It's easy for us to approach a command like this as something that God would never *actually* ask of us. We know He's not actually going to have us sacrifice our children.

And yet God asks things of us every day that we dismiss. He asks us to

- Forgive our enemies.
- Love those who persecute us.
- Tithe ten percent of our income.
- Give control of our lives to Jesus.
- Pray without ceasing.

When you know Christ, you know these commands are not unthinkable. Rather, they are unquestionably the wisest and most liberating actions we can take. They are godly responses to life, and they elevate our thinking, our relationships, and our ability to address situations at levels unattainable outside of this kind of obedience.

Second, there is always more to what God says than what we initially understand. God's words are always filled with the infinite because He is infinite. To think He gives us quick, superficial directives that have not been thought through reveals some not-so-positive realities about us.

We are arrogant to suggest we think things through more than God does, and that what He says is shallow and full of holes. We are foolish if we ignore His commands, assuming our ways are better than His ways. We are lost if we think we can draw a better map for our lives than God can.

Third, the desires of your heart will eventually line up with the things God has for you—to the point that you will be overjoyed and blessed when God comes through. Think about Abraham. He was at a point in his life at which he was sure he would be childless for the rest of his life. And God changed all that. God's plan for Abraham's life brought a completion and a joy that Abraham might never have thought to ask for on his own. In addition, Abraham now understood something about himself—that he would hold nothing back from God. Isaac now understood that too! What a great parenting lesson that was for Isaac. I wonder what their conversation was like on the way down the mountain.

Too often, we assume that following God means being forced to live a way that won't be desirable to us. But that's simply not true. God changes the heart; He impacts your desires, so you will love what He loves.

Put Your Trust Where Your Heart Is

Too often we don't trust God enough to "try" what He is telling us to do, and we miss out.

When you trust somebody, you're willing to try new things. But when there's a lack of trust, you're not so quick to jump in.

If you've got a muddy pool of water, and somebody says, "Go ahead, jump in, you're safe," you probably aren't going to jump, no matter how confident that person sounds. You aren't going to jump, because you can't see what you're jumping into! So, your likelihood of following through is completely based on whether or not you trust the person telling you to jump.

When we walk with the Lord, we don't see everything. Yet when He says, "Jump!" we have to trust.

We learn to trust by giving things over to Him.

Sometimes it's a slow process. Every day, we give a little bit here and a little bit there. It's like learning to trust anybody; we give ourselves over to that person bit by bit. As he or she shows himself or herself to be trustworthy, then we give more and more.

But the Lord doesn't just want a small part of us. The Lord says, "I want all of you." You may not always feel you have the means to do what God says, but you've got to have the heart to be *willing* to do what He says.

Abraham was not sitting around the house with his bags packed, waiting for God to tell him to sacrifice his son. But his heart was ready to do whatever God asked him to do. And when that request came, Abraham responded. He went to the mountain prepared with fire, wood, and a knife. He went to the mountain set on doing God's will.

We have no idea about some of the things God will ask of us as time rolls on. But we need to be prepared, and we need to decide now that whatever the request, the answer will be yes.

Prayer

Lord, show me any things, any areas of my life that I am holding back from You.

I ask that You would give me the courage to say "yes" to those commands that You put before me. I ask to experience a level of freedom that is unattainable outside of You—for the courage to make those decisions.

Lord, I know I can't really grasp the emotions and the angst that surrounded Abraham's willingness to sacrifice his son. Yet I know that You have asked much less of me, and I still battle to come through for You. Help me in this, I pray. I want to change.

I thank You, Lord, that You came, and You lived, and You died—for us. You rose from the dead so that we can live.

I pray in Christ's name, amen.

WORKBOOK

Chapter Two Questions

Question: What in your life, if anything, would you hold back from God if He asked you for it?

_____

_____

_____

_____

_____

_____

_____

_____

_____

_____

_____

Question: Are you ready to obey God when He guides you, or do you first reason, argue, or complain about His commands? What is the link between obedience and trust?

_____

_____

_____

_____

_____

_____

_____

_____

_____

_____

Question: Looking back over your life, can you see how God's direction and your desires have come to align themselves? Give an example of a time something seemed unbearable but was really leading you closer to the desires of your heart.

_____

_____

_____

_____

_____

_____

_____

_____

_____

_____

_____

_____

Action: Write out a list of things that seem unthinkable—these could be difficult commands from Scripture or things you've said you would "never do" (e.g., move to a certain place, give someone a second chance, encourage your child to enter a certain occupation). Pray for God to give you a willing heart to do whatever He asks of you. Then, at the top of your list, write "unquestionably yes."

_____

_____

_____

_____

_____

_____

_____

_____

Chapter Two Notes

_____

_____

_____

_____

_____

_____

_____

_____

_____

_____

_____

_____

_____

_____

_____

_____

_____

_____

_____

_____

_____

_____

_____

CHAPTER THREE

Lead My People!

But Moses said to God, "Who am I, that I should go to Pharaoh and bring the Israelites out of Egypt?"
—Exodus 3:11

Have you ever had someone come to you and ask for help? It might have been something minor, such as to borrow your lawn mower or some tool. Or it might have been a little more involved, like taking care of the person's pet for a couple of weeks. Or maybe it was more significant, such as people asking you to watch their kids while they take a trip.

Most people ask for help at some time or another. Those who refuse to ask for help believe that they are self-sufficient and, frankly, they are a bit prideful. Nonetheless, we all need help at times, whether we request it or not.

It is frustrating when we have someone ask for help but he or she refuses to accept the help we offer. I've had people through the years come by the church and ask for gas money or money for food or other needs. It is not uncommon that when we offer to take them to a gas station, or give them actual food, they get upset. Why? Because they want the money! They really don't want help; they want money to do what they want to do.

I also know from personal experience that sometimes we don't like the advice we're given. I've been given instructions that I didn't follow at times because I thought I knew better, but I didn't.

Sometimes we resist because we perceive God's command to be absurd and outrageous. How could God demand that Abraham sacrifice his only son? How could He command Noah to complete the outlandish task of building an ark and stocking it with every kind of animal on earth?

Remember, God's absurd, outrageous commands are meant to help us meet challenges. They bring life and character and blessings, however hard they may be in the walking out.

Moses, when he was the prince of Egypt, looked on the plight of the Israelites and hurt for them. After all, he was one of them. He disdained their abuse at the hands of the Egyptians. In fact, he even murdered an Egyptian in an effort to protect the Israelites. As a result, Moses became a fugitive, ultimately relegated to the backside of the desert, no longer a prince of Egypt but now relegated to exist as a lowly nomadic shepherd (Exodus 2:11–14).

However, that didn't mean there wasn't something still burning deep in his soul for the people he had left behind, and God knew it. After all, it was God who had planted the passion for the redemption of the Israelites in his heart.

So, God came to Moses in the desert and revealed Himself and His plan to His chosen servant:

> Now Moses was tending the flock of Jethro his father-in-law, the priest of Midian, and he led the flock to the far side of the wilderness and came to Horeb, the mountain of God. There the angel of the LORD appeared to him in flames of fire from within a bush. Moses saw that though the bush was on fire it did not burn up. So Moses thought, "I will go over and see this strange sight—why the bush does not burn up."
>
> When the LORD saw that he had gone over to look, God called to him from within the bush, "Moses! Moses!"
>
> And Moses said, "Here I am."
>
> "Do not come any closer," God said. "Take off your sandals, for the place where you are standing is holy ground." Then he said, "I am the God of your father,] the God of Abraham, the God of Isaac and the God of Jacob." At this, Moses hid his face, because he was afraid to look at God.
>
> The LORD said, "I have indeed seen the misery of my people in Egypt. I have heard them crying out because of their slave drivers, and I am concerned about their suffering. So I have come down to rescue them from the hand of the Egyptians and to bring them up out of that land into a good and spacious land, a land flowing with milk and honey—the home of the Canaanites, Hittites, Amorites, Perizzites, Hivites and Jebusites. And now the cry of the Israelites has reached me, and I have seen the way the Egyptians are oppressing them. So now, go. I am sending you to Pharaoh to bring my people the Israelites out of Egypt."
>
> —*Exodus 3:1-10*

You'd think Moses would dance with joy. Not only did he have a chance to rise out of obscurity, but he could also be instrumental in leading his people out of slavery.

Yet he balked. It sounded absurd! Moses' vision was clouded by his doubts and fears. He had grown comfortable in his complacency.

Most of us, if not all of us, want to make a difference in this life. We want to make a mark that leaves a positive impression on the world. But, all too often, we grow comfortable in our circumstances and in our lives. The barrier between you and making a difference in your life is your pushback on God. Are you ready to push forward instead of pushing back?

Road Signs from God

We need to learn some important lessons from this chapter of Moses' life. Let's take note of some clear principles that are set forth in this passage of Scripture.

What you are doing may only be a precursor to something else that God has for you. Moses was tending sheep. While Moses, at one time, had been a prince, he later became a shepherd. Being a prince, somehow, seems more romantic and desirable.

- Princes lead people. Shepherds lead sheep.

- Princes eat at the king's table. Shepherds eat with the animals.

- Princes have a staff of attendants. Shepherds have a staff.

- Princes have privilege. Shepherds have poverty.

Moses' life embraced both of these positions, and God had a special call for him. He raised him as a leader, taught him as a shepherd, and now expected him to lead His people out of Egypt and shepherd them through the desert. Moses might have thought that his calling was merely to shepherd sheep, but that was only a precursor to what God ultimately had for him.

What are you currently doing with your life? Where do you think God is leading you? What unique call has He given you that is causing you to push back instead of push forward?

Miracles—like a burning bush—are given to get your attention, not dominate your pursuits. A bush was on fire, but the fire did not consume the bush. It didn't make sense. God knows how to get our attention.

But the point wasn't that there was a bush burning without being consumed. The point was for Moses to answer God's call to lead the people out of Egypt. Miracles aren't ends in themselves. They are road signs that point to God. What have been the miracles in your lives?

- Was it the birth of your little baby?
- Was it surviving that financial pressure cooker?
- Was it finding that job that you love?
- Was it finding new love in your marriage?

- Was it the healing of a loved family member?

What has God done to get your attention? Have you allowed that miracle to point you to Christ and help you listen to what He has to say? Or has the miracle become an end in itself, and all you can talk about is what God did instead of recognizing what He wants to do in you and through you?

God won't ignore you when you look in His direction. Have you ever wondered what would have happened if Moses, after seeing the burning bush, instead of going to it, turned back and was satisfied with telling his wife about it? He would have gone no further than that.

Instead, Moses pushed toward the miracle. He didn't ignore God's attempt to get his attention. I wonder how many of us have ignored God's attempts to get our attention, and then complained or wondered later why God seemed to be ignoring us.

Humbling ourselves before God doesn't always mean that we lose all fear. Some fear is healthy. Moses knew to act. He didn't hesitate. He took off his sandals. He got it. Why? There was still some fear in him. He knew that God was not someone with whom to trifle. And he willingly humbled himself before God.

We often need to be reminded of the power of God. It is not bad to maintain a healthy fear of God—a fear that embraces reverence and some level of trepidation. Who God is makes us stop and think.

Healthy fear is a staple of life. While we don't live in fear, possessing it helps to protect us from danger. It keeps us alert and helps us to become better listeners. What is your attitude when you approach God? Do you recognize His power? It's good that you understand His love and His grace and His forgiveness. It's good that you marinate in His presence and revel in His glory. But if you forget His power, you're apt to become more complacent in your walk with Him.

The unexpected is always followed by what is expected of us. God had a job for Moses to do. It wasn't about a bush that didn't burn; it was about a people that didn't have hope. When God does the unexpected, it's not for show; He is headed somewhere.

Once you have experienced the unexpected from God, have you responded by doing what He expects? What are you doing that demonstrates that Jesus is genuinely your Savior and Lord? What difference are you making? Are you too busy pushing back to make a difference? Or are you too busy making excuses? God has expectations of you. Don't overlook that.

Your pushback on God's direction in your life creates barriers, not escape routes. Moses was filled with excuses as to why he couldn't do what God was calling him to do. He was drawn to the miracle. He was humbled in God's presence. He recognized God's power. But he resisted God's will. What is God asking of you? Why are you pushing back? Don't construct barriers or be content to ignore God's call upon your life.

Most of us, if not all of us, want to make a difference in life. We want to make a mark that leaves a positive impression on the world. But, all too often, we have grown comfortable in our circumstances and in life. We think that when God steps in to give us direction, moving us out of our comfortable place, He is being absurd. So, we push back.

The barrier between you and a difference in your life is your pushback on God. Are you ready to push forward instead of pushing back? Are you ready to obey the absurd, outrageous command of God?

Prayer

God, You know I desire to make a difference. But sometimes what's required seems so outrageous. Please help me to pay attention to You, to truly listen to You, to be humble and rightfully fearful before You. Help me see what direction the miracles in my life are pointing me to. Help me do the job You are calling me to do, no matter how absurd it seems. I want to follow Your call. In Jesus' name, amen.

WORKBOOK

Chapter Three Questions

Question: What are some areas in which you long to make a difference? Are there ways in which complacency has overtaken your desires and dreams?

_____

_____

_____

_____

_____

_____

_____

_____

_____

_____

_____

Question: Have you witnessed a miracle in your life? How did God use it to get your attention?

_____

_____

_____

_____

_____

_____

_____

_____

_____

_____

_____

Question: What are examples of healthy fears? What does it mean to fear God?

_____

_____

_____

_____

_____

_____

_____

_____

_____

_____

_____

_____

Action: Scripture is full of stories of men and women who, like Moses, went through a time of preparation before taking on the world-changing ministry God intended for them. Do a study on the "wilderness years" of Joseph, Moses, David, Jesus, or Paul. How did God use this time of faithfulness in obscurity to prepare them for what lay ahead?

Chapter Three Notes

_____

_____

_____

_____

_____

_____

_____

_____

_____

_____

_____

_____

_____

_____

_____

_____

_____

_____

_____

_____

_____

_____

CHAPTER FOUR

Have a Parade!

Then the LORD said to Joshua, "See, I have delivered Jericho into your hands, along with its king and its fighting men. March around the city once with all the armed men. Do this for six days.

—Joshua 6:2–3

I remember my first varsity wrestling match in high school. During weigh-in, I was sizing up my opponent. He was shorter than I was and considerably more muscular. I was tall and skinny.

As I thought about it, I found myself becoming a bit intimidated. *Can I beat him? He is surely a lot stronger than I am.* My mind was swimming in doubt. It wasn't long before the time came, and we met in the middle of the mat.

The whistle blew, and the day of reckoning had arrived. I moved in and grabbed his neck. To my surprise, I was stronger than he was. Not only that, but I was quicker, too. I won my first varsity wrestling match that day. I was on top of the world!

We've all been in situations where we thought the odds were against us, that nothing we possessed was going take us over the top.

I imagine Joshua felt the same way when God told him to take the city of Jericho. But, instead of wallowing in self-doubt, instead of protesting at such an absurd, outrageous command, he went for it. Joshua answered the call in the face of all odds.

That's faith. It's persistence in the face of overwhelming odds. There is a tenacity to it. Faith says "yes" to the absurd and outrageous when it comes from God.

Not Your Typical Battle Strategy

Joshua 5 tells the story of the Israelites crossing the Jordan River. God had dried it up to allow them to pass— an incredible thing! Word got out, and the surrounding cities and kings were terrified, because it was clear that Yahweh was with Israel.

Chapter 6 is where the battle of Jericho picks up:

> Now the gates of Jericho were securely barred because of the Israelites. No one went out and no one came in.
>
> Then the LORD said to Joshua, "See, I have delivered Jericho into your hands, along with its king and its fighting men. March around the city once with all the armed men. Do this for six days. Have seven priests carry trumpets of rams' horns in front of the ark. On the seventh day, march around the city seven times, with the priests blowing the trumpets. When you hear them sound a long blast on the trumpets, have the whole army give a loud shout; then the

wall of the city will collapse and the army will go up, everyone straight in."

So Joshua son of Nun called the priests and said to them, "Take up the ark of the covenant of the LORD and have seven priests carry trumpets in front of it." And he ordered the army, "Advance! March around the city, with an armed guard going ahead of the ark of the LORD."

When Joshua had spoken to the people, the seven priests carrying the seven trumpets before the LORD went forward, blowing their trumpets, and the ark of the LORD's covenant followed them. The armed guard marched ahead of the priests who blew the trumpets, and the rear guard followed the ark. All this time the trumpets were sounding. But Joshua had commanded the army, "Do not give a war cry, do not raise your voices, do not say a word until the day I tell you to shout. Then shout!" So he had the ark of the LORD carried around the city, circling it once. Then the army returned to camp and spent the night there.

Joshua got up early the next morning and the priests took up the ark of the LORD. The seven priests carrying the seven trumpets went forward, marching before the ark of the LORD and blowing the trumpets. The armed men went ahead of them and the rear guard followed the ark of the LORD, while the trumpets kept sounding. So on the second day they marched around the city once and returned to the camp. They did this for six days.

—Joshua 6:1–14

I'm going to pause here to address just how absurd and outrageous this whole thing is. First, Joshua was told that, in order to conquer a city, he had to march around it. And, if that wasn't ridiculous enough, he had to be completely silent. No war cries. No posturing. Just some trumpets and some marching.

Do you think Joshua had his doubts? It's possible. But whatever concerns or questions he had, he pushed those aside and did what God asked.

On the seventh day, they got up at daybreak and marched around the city seven times in the same manner, except that on that day they circled the city seven times. The seventh time around, when the priests sounded the trumpet blast, Joshua commanded the army, "Shout! For the LORD has given you the city! The city and all that is in it are to be devoted to the LORD. Only Rahab the prostitute and all who are with her in her house shall be spared, because she hid the spies we sent. But keep away from the devoted things, so that you will not bring about your own destruction by taking any of them. Otherwise you will make the camp of Israel liable to destruction and bring trouble on it. All the silver and gold and the articles of bronze and iron are sacred to the LORD and must go into his treasury."

When the trumpets sounded, the army shouted, and at the sound of the trumpet, when the men gave a loud shout, the wall collapsed; so everyone charged straight in, and they took the city.

—Joshua 6:15–20

No matter how outrageous or absurd the command was, it worked.

There are times we may be fearful about stepping out. We may be certain that we don't stand a chance if we follow what God wants us to do. But we need to remember there is a power beyond us at work.

"Am I on God's Side?"

The Israelites weren't skilled warriors. They were nomads. They'd been wandering the desert for forty years.

They didn't have practice with military drills or sacking cities, let alone scaling walls. Everything they did was through the strength and will of God, and then *boom*. They were faced with the city of Jericho.

UNESCO says that the Jericho walls and tower were the "earliest urban fortifications known in the world."[3] So imagine that: not only were the Israelites unskilled warriors, but they were going up against one of the best-fortified cities in the entire world.

Scaling the smooth-stoned walls would be nearly impossible without ladders or some kind of equipment. Plus, getting even close to the walls was a danger, as they would be vulnerable to attack. It's easy to assume that God's people felt a bit outmatched.

Now, God had been leading the Israelites to this Promised Land, so it couldn't have been a complete shock that they were to overtake a city to claim their reward. But *this* city? The one with the huge walls?

That might have been a surprise, but it probably wasn't as surprising as being visited by an angel of the Lord.

> Now when Joshua was near Jericho, he looked up and saw a man standing in front of him with a drawn sword in his hand. Joshua went up to him and asked, "Are you for us or for our enemies?"
>
> "Neither," he replied, "but as commander of the army of the LORD I have now come." Then Joshua fell facedown to the ground in reverence, and asked him, "What message does my LORD have for his servant?"
>
> The commander of the LORD's army replied, "Take off your sandals, for the place where you are standing is holy." And

Joshua did so.

—Joshua 5:13–15

Can you imagine? Joshua was in the middle of dealing with the reality of overtaking a city (after wandering in the desert for forty years, I might add); then, he came face to face with the commander of the Lord's army.

If that isn't a confidence-booster, then I don't know what is. It's no wonder that Joshua followed God's directive—move for move.

Joshua was in a position where he had to listen, not to what his doubts might tell him or even to what some of his officers might tell him, but his only aim was to listen to the Lord and move forward.

When things are difficult, we sometimes wonder, "Is God on my side?" But that's the wrong way of looking at it. Instead, we should ask whether we're on God's side.

Leaning on God

I entered the ministry at twenty years old as a youth pastor. I stayed there for three years, and then, at the age of twenty-three, I took my first church as a senior pastor. It was a thing of God, because that church had been looking for someone who was older and more experienced. They wanted a pastor in the middle or near the end of his career—not someone whose only experience was leading teens to summer camp and running pie-eating contests at youth group.

Can you say "wet behind the ears"? My ears were dripping!

I remember sitting down in my first counseling session. I was listening as the person opened their heart and poured out everything they were going through. They barely knew me, and yet they gave me a level of trust, as if I'd been their pastor for the last ten years.

I was deeply affected by that. I had done nothing to earn their trust except to say "yes" to the pastor position and then sit down in the chair across from them. I kept wondering what I could offer them. What did I have that they needed? What could I possibly do to help when I'd only known them for such a short time?

It turned out to be one of the greatest lessons in my life. As I sat there, I realized that they didn't need my life experience. They needed my God experience. They needed truths from the Scripture and the Word of the Lord.

It is not our experience with the crisis that matters; it's our experience with God. If we know Him, and if we're listening to and trusting Him, He will work through us. He'll teach us. He'll take us to levels we would never attain outside of Him. He gives us insight and wisdom that is unattainable, separate from Him.

Life is full of crises and trouble, there's no doubt about it. But we don't need to cower in the corner. We don't need to let our lack of experience convince us that we can't contribute meaningfully toward resolution.

As the story of Jericho shows, our main hurdle isn't the wall that exists between us and our problems. The main hurdle is the wall between us and God.

When we knock this wall down, when we choose to remove whatever stands between us and our Lord, then every single wall that comes after is scalable. Every enemy is defeatable. Every problem is solvable, because God, in all of His power and wisdom and knowledge, will give us the direction we need.

People of faith don't lean on their own experience. They lean on the experience and the presence of God. In other words, it's not our methods that win the battle; it's our willingness to walk by faith and exercise *God's* methods—no matter how absurd or outrageous.

A Method to the Madness

The story of the battle of Jericho is incredible proof of what can happen when inexperienced people trust God to fill in the gaps.

God was very specific in how He wanted Israel to conquer Jericho. Joshua 6:4 says, "Have seven priests carry trumpets of rams' horns in front of the ark. On the seventh day, march around the city seven times, with the priests blowing the trumpets."

Now, at face value, these directives seem pretty crazy! But there was a lot of meaning to them. *Seven* appears throughout the Bible, and it is seen as God's perfect number. *Priests* were advocates who went to God on behalf of the people. So, having seven priests leading the people was very symbolic. God wanted seven advocates to lead the way.

Another significant detail is the rams' horns. These horns were blown to call the people to worship and whenever a sacrifice had taken place.

So, when you have seven priests, who are advocates

for the people, and they're blowing seven rams' horns, representing atonement, salvation, and victory, then you've got a pretty special mix. And for them to do this for seven days? The meaning behind it is incredible.

God could have called a lot more people to blow horns and lead the march—that certainly would have been more intimidating to the civilians within the city walls. But God chose seven. *Seven.* It wasn't about intimidation. It was about giving glory to God.

And if you think about it, there was nothing difficult about the directives. All they had to do was walk. A few had to blow some horns. The rest had to stay quiet. That was it. How easy, compared to most battle strategies!

We've heard many of the Bible's commands over and over, and many of them aren't that absurd or outrageous: Love God. Love your neighbor. Don't lie, steal, cheat. Don't be proud. Care for the less fortunate. Give to the needy. These aren't difficult commands. They're basic, really. So why is it so hard to follow them?

We tend to blow things out of proportion. We get emotional about stuff. We think selfishly instead of selflessly. And whenever we're focused on ourselves, that's when it's hard to have faith. It's hard to do the right thing. It's hard to hear God.

The walls of Jericho were not the ultimate challenge. Your relationships, pain, addiction, and temptations are not the ultimate challenge. The ultimate challenge is: "Are we going to trust God to come through for us?"

Finish the Battle!

Every day that Israel marched, nothing seemed to change. The walls didn't start to crumble. The stone didn't crack. And the people inside Jericho certainly didn't start to open the gates in surrender. Yet Israel still marched. The Israelites continued on, because that's what God told them to do.

There may have been times when their faith waned a bit. Times when they thought Joshua was crazy. Times when they thought *they* were crazy.

And yet, they walked. It was an utterly simple act, and yet it meant everything. It was a physical representation of the faith they ultimately had in their Creator.

And then day seven came. They walked. They blew horns. And then the walls shook and cracked and shifted. And the people stood watching as the walls crumbled to the ground.

I wonder how many times you and I have been cheated out of significant miracles because we didn't see things through to the end. Partway through, we decided we weren't going to do it. We decided it wasn't worth it— that God wasn't worth it. We quit.

We might have gone around telling others that we had tried to follow God, doing what He said, but it didn't work for us, it was just too outrageous. *Because He never came through.*

But the reality was that *we* never did what God said. *We* never came through.

We did parts of things, sure, but we never finished the journey. We never went all in. We dropped out on the sixth day of marching. And, consequently, we missed everything that God had planned for us.

It's easy to get fired up and excited about what could be and all the *what-ifs* that are out there. But it's a lot harder to do the work. To engage when God says it's go time. To get off our butts and give ourselves over to Him. To trust Him for immeasurably more.

Even when the directive is as simple as walking around a city, it can be hard.

But something has to change. We have to get our minds on the right stuff. It's not about us. It's not about feeling comfortable and protecting ourselves and only giving God a small bit. It's about giving it all to Him and *knowing* that it will be worth it.

Have you experienced God enough to *know* that He is with you? That He is more than qualified to take care of anything that comes before you?

So, don't give up. Keep a willing spirit. Keep marching. Keep moving forward by the power of the Holy Spirit until the victories are won.

For it's not by our strength or by what we have within ourselves that the battles are won. It's through God that we see victory. It's through faith and obedience—even when He asks us to do the absurd and the outrageous.

Prayer

Lord, there have been times when I've been in the battle, and it just wasn't going the way I thought it should. Instead of doing what You called me to do, I just stopped. I missed the victory.

I know I don't always understand what You tell me to do. Your directives don't always make sense to me. But please help me to stay in the battle. Help me to remember that if I don't do what You ask and follow through, then I won't experience victory.

Thank You for Your faithfulness. May I commit to You through the long haul. May I be willing to obey whatever command You give me.

To You belong the honor and the glory, in Christ's name. Amen.

WORKBOOK

Chapter Four Questions

Question: From a human standpoint, did the odds favor Jericho or Israel? Why? When have you been in a situation in which the odds were stacked against you?

_____

_____

_____

_____

_____

_____

_____

_____

_____

_____

Question: What are some of the "enemies" that keep you from victory in Christ? What evidence in your life shows that you trust God to overcome these challenges?

_____

_____

_____

_____

_____

_____

_____

_____

_____

_____

_____

Question: *It is not our experience with the crisis that matters; it's our experience with God.* When has God used you to minister in a crisis that was beyond your experience? How were you able to encourage others through the Lord and His Word?

_____

_____

_____

_____

_____

_____

_____

_____

_____

_____

_____

_____

Action: Create a sign with the words "Just Keep March-ing" and put it in a place where you will see it often and be reminded not to give up or slack off in obedience while you wait for God to come through for you.

Chapter Four Notes

CHAPTER FIVE

Trim Down Your Army!

The LORD said to Gideon, "You have too many men for me to deliver Midian into their hands. In order that Israel may not boast against me that her own strength has saved her, announce now to the people, 'Anyone who trembles with fear may turn back and leave Mount Gilead.'"
—*Judges 7:2–3a*

At the battle of Gettysburg, Colonel Joshua Lawrence Chamberlain of Maine and his troops were responsible for defending a hill called Little Round Top. If they lost the hill, the Confederate army could have swept in from behind and potentially defeated the Union army.

The battle raged for hours. Colonel Chamberlain's men were outnumbered and almost out of ammunition. Knowing he couldn't give up the hill, Chamberlain gave his men an absurd and outrageous order: "Fix your bayonets and charge downhill to the enemy."

What was so absurd about that? No army with any sense would attack with only bayonets without a vast army behind them. The move was a bold bluff to trick the Rebels into assuming that many more troops were right behind Chamberlain's men. And the bluff worked. The Confederates turned and ran, and Chamberlain's men took hundreds of prisoners.

In fact, legend holds that Chamberlain approached a Union private who was holding about a dozen prisoners with his rifle. The private said, "Colonel, I don't have a bullet in my gun." Chamberlain whispered to the private: "Not so loud, soldier."[4] Talk about outrageous!

You and I are on a faith trek, taking a look at the absurd, outrageous commands of God. We've looked at a few of them already. In this chapter, we will look at another absurd, outrageous command of God found in the book of Judges, given to a person by the name of Gideon. The absurd command? For Gideon to trim down his already outnumbered and out-equipped army.

Understand, it's not the strength of our human resources that brings the victory; it is our trust in God. It's believing that He has the ability to take us through whatever is before us—however outrageous His instructions may seem.

God Is Our Strength

The story of Gideon actually unfolds in Judges 6–8. But first, let's look at some historical background for this story so that we know what is really happening.

The book of Judges relates the period of Israel's history when there was no king. The basic plot of the book is a cycle: The people would turn their backs on God, and as punishment for their rebellion, God would send a different group of people that would basically conquer, attack, and harass them. God would then put a judge into power who, by the power of the Holy Spirit, would lead the people to victory over their oppressors and reestablish peace in the nation.

There were fifteen judges (if you count Eli, the high priest, and Samuel, the prophet, who entered the scene at the end of the book). Gideon was the fifth of these judges.

> The angel of the LORD came and sat down under the oak in Ophrah that belonged to Joash the Abiezrite, where his son Gideon was threshing wheat in a winepress to keep it from the Midianites. When the angel of the LORD appeared to Gideon, he said, "The Lord is with you, mighty warrior."
>
> "Pardon me, my lord," Gideon replied, "but if the LORD is with us, why has all this happened to us? Where are all his wonders that our ancestors told us about when they said, 'Did not the LORD bring us up out of Egypt?' But now the LORD has abandoned us and given us into the hand of Midian."
>
> The LORD turned to him and said, "Go in the strength you have and save Israel out of Midian's hand. Am I not sending you?"
>
> "Pardon me, my lord," Gideon replied, "but how can I save Israel? My clan is the weakest in Manasseh, and I am the least in my family."
>
> The LORD answered, "I will be with you, and you will strike down all the Midianites, leaving none alive."
> —*Judges 6:11–16*

The first verse of this chapter started like every other

prelude to an Israelite judge in this book: "Again, the Israelites did evil in the sight of the LORD" (Judges 6:1). So, here they were, right back into rebellion, in spite of having been liberated four times already.

Now they were oppressed by the Midianites, a nomadic people with a powerful army. Each year following the harvest, hordes of Midianites rampaged Israelite land and completely plundered it. They'd done this enough years that now the Israelites were hiding in caves and starving. They were terrorized and living in utter fear.

This is where we find Gideon—hiding in a winepress, threshing wheat, trying to do his job without being discovered. And an angel of the Lord came up to him, greeting him with a title that surely felt like a mistake, if not a mockery, to the cowering Israelite: "Greetings, mighty warrior."

You and I would never have looked at Gideon and called him a mighty warrior.

But God doesn't just see us for who we are. He also sees us for who we can become. He sees who we can become, not on our own, but by His power. He sees who He's called us to be.

The Israelites didn't have a shot, but they did have a prayer. They had the hope God could do something beyond the norm.

Who You're With Counts

Now, we can take three simple lessons from this. What do we learn from Gideon? First, it is not a matter of who you are; it is a matter of who you are with.

We see in Scripture and throughout time, God does not call extraordinary people. Those aren't the ones He really wants—they're the ones *we* want. Instead, He calls ordinary people who don't necessarily stand out in a crowd.

Take, for example, when Israel's first king came along. They didn't need a king, but Israel thought they did because everybody else had one, and Israel chose Saul. God didn't choose Saul. Israel chose Saul because he stood out in the crowd.

God typically doesn't choose people who stand out in a crowd. He chooses people off to the side or those whom others reject. The apostle Paul marveled at this. He said:

> *Brothers and sisters, think of what you were when you were called. Not many of you were wise by human standards; not many were influential; not many were of noble birth. But God chose the foolish things of the world to shame the wise; God chose the weak things of the world to shame the strong.*
>
> **—1 Corinthians 1:26–27**

One thing I deal with all the time, and I suspect you do as well, is coming face to face with my own inadequacy. I wonder, "How can I even pastor? How can I do what God has asked me to do, because I know where I am weak and where I continually fall on my face. I know what I am unable to do—and it is a whole lot."

Our inadequacies just glare at us. Quite honestly, if we did not recognize our inadequacies, we wouldn't pursue God. It's coming face to face with those inadequacies, and understanding that we are nothing, in and of ourselves, that helps us lean on the Lord and trust Him.

Look at this scripture: "Not that we are adequate in ourselves to consider anything as coming from ourselves, but our adequacy is from God..." (2 Corinthians 3:5 NASB). When that truth settles in, that is when we become mighty warriors, valiant warriors. We become men and women of God who are able to do what we could never do by our own strength.

It is interesting to see what is written in verse 34 in the book of Judges. It says, "The spirit of the LORD came upon Gideon" (Judges 6:34). Literally, in Hebrew, it means: "The Spirit of the LORD clothed Himself with Gideon." What does that mean? It means God indwelt Gideon. He put him on until the power of who Gideon was, was God Himself.

Maybe we ought to pray differently and say, "Lord, put me on today as Your suit. Wear me, so that wherever I go, it's not me, it's You. May the substance of my life and what gives me hope and what gives me victory be Your power and Your work within me. You are my adequacy."

Hudson Taylor, who founded the China Inland Mission, said: "All of God's great men have been weak men who did great things for God because they reckoned on His power being with them."[5] Not because they were great. But because God is great. And despite what happens around us, we will come to the point where we can say, "God did it; it isn't me."

Whom Do You Run To?

Just as it's not about who you are, but who you're with,

it's also not about what you're running from, but whom you're running *to*.

Gideon didn't really get it. Rather than muster up an army, he went home—to a home that was rampant with idol worship.

Gideon was struggling. He knew God had called him, but he was still scared. He knew he needed to tear down the idols. He even had specific instructions to sacrifice the prime bull (Gideon 6:25–26). It was time for that bull that had sired all those Baal sacrifices to be sacrificed himself.

Well, the townspeople weren't too keen on Gideon's behavior. So, they gathered outside Gideon's dad's home and demanded that Gideon come out. But Gideon's dad defended him: If Baal was truly god, he told the towns-people, he would take care of Gideon.

The people agreed that this was a good point—which meant, from that time forward, whenever those people saw Gideon, they were reminded of the weakness of Baal and the power of God. All in one person.

We need to understand that, when we walk with God in obedience, we represent not only the power of God, but also the weakness of Satan. He didn't win. He didn't conquer us. He doesn't own us. It's not simply what we are running from—it is whom we are running to, and we are running to the Lord.

I think part of our struggle in our walk with God is that we don't take the steps Gideon took. When we walk with the Lord, we say, "Okay, Lord, I want to walk with You. I've got to tackle my sin." Or, "I have got this addiction over here," and so we go after the sin or the addiction, when the first step should be to go after God. We must pursue Him first.

That's what Gideon was getting at. No, it is not the Midianites first. We seek God first. We restore Him as the King, as the Ruler.

It's Not About Victory—It's About Trust

God is not merely interested in giving us the victory. He is concerned with teaching us to trust Him. I think we are prone to assume we know what the answers ought to be when we seek wisdom from God in the midst of our struggles. We say, "God, this is what the answer looks like, in case You are in the dark about it." But God is saying, "No, this is what the answer looks like."

Can we trust that His answer is better than ours? That the way He addresses a problem is more substantive than ours? Let's read on to see how Gideon learned this lesson.

Gideon mustered up an army of 32,000 men (Judges 7:3)—against a Midianite army of 135,000. As he marched toward battle, imagine the dialogue between Gideon and the Lord going something like this:

God: Gideon, we have a problem here.

Gideon: You bet we do—there are 32,000 of us and 135,000 of them.

God: I know. Your army is too big. We need to trim it down.

Gideon: What? That's absurd!

God: First, any of your soldiers who are scared may go

home.

Gideon: Are You serious? You know that describes, like, 22,000 of us.

God: Yes.

Gideon's army dwindles to 10,000.

A little later...

God: We still have a problem.

Gideon: Yeah. And it's getting bigger.

God: You still have too many soldiers.

Gideon: You're not serious.

God: Do this. Go to the springs of Harad and have your soldiers get a drink. The ones who lap up the water like a dog, send them home. The ones who cup water in their hands to drink, keep those.

Gideon's army shrinks to three hundred.

God: Finally, we have an army here!

As if a measly band of three hundred cup-drinking Israelites isn't absurd enough, the Lord gave Gideon further outrageous commands on how to defeat the dreaded Midianites: Each soldier was to be armed with an empty clay pitcher, a torch, and a trumpet. Around ten thirty at night the Israelites broke their clay pitchers, lit their torches, and blew their trumpets.

The Midianites were absolutely gripped with fear. Scripture records they turned and killed each other and ran. God brought this incredible victory to the Israelites.

Trimming down your army when you're already out-matched—absurd! Attacking the enemy with dishes and flashlights and trumpets—outrageous!

For Gideon, the answer was simple obedience. Just do what you know to do and let God take care of the rest.

God still calls His troops into battle against over-whelming odds. Are you ready to follow? God always asks us to do things we can't, because He wants to show us who He is with His nature, strength, provision, and kindness to us and to the world.

Make sure you are ready and willing to tap in to the power of God in your life. God is at work, and He wants all of us trusting Him. It's not the strength of your human resources that brings the victory; it's your faith in God.

Prayer

Father, when we see You work, we recognize it. And so often, just like the Israelites, we forget and we return to our old ways. We don't want to do that. So, Lord, we are going to do our part. We are going to trust You and lean on You. And by Your Spirit, our trust will expand and Your Word will go out. Lord, anybody You are tapping on the shoulder, I pray they would step up to You, surrender their lives, and be a part of the great work You are doing for Your glory. We pray this in Your most holy name, amen.

WORKBOOK

Chapter Five Questions

Question: Why does God so often choose ordinary and insignificant people through which to do great things?

_____

_____

_____

_____

_____

_____

_____

_____

_____

_____

_____

Question: How does your life demonstrate both the power of God and the weakness of Satan?

_____

_____

_____

_____

_____

_____

_____

_____

_____

_____

_____

Question: How did Gideon demonstrate his faith in God? What specifically can you do today to live out your faith?

_____

_____

_____

_____

_____

_____

_____

_____

_____

_____

_____

_____

Action: Read Hebrews 11. Write down every example of a person who obeyed, in faith, an "outrageous" command of God.

_____

_____

_____

_____

_____

_____

_____

_____

_____

_____

_____

Chapter Five Notes

_____

_____

_____

_____

_____

_____

_____

_____

_____

_____

_____

_____

_____

_____

_____

_____

_____

_____

_____

_____

_____

_____

_____

CHAPTER SIX

Have a Baby!

You will conceive and give birth to a son, and you are to call him Jesus.
—Luke 1:31

Have you ever felt that God put you in a jam? That He put you in a lose-lose situation? That He trapped you into doing something you never, ever would have wanted to do?

I think we all feel this way at times. I've talked with many who assumed or believed that, in the midst of the chaos, God forgot, abandoned, and/or toyed with them.

But God is all-knowing. And when He "puts us in a jam," it's because He has big things planned.

It's not always easy to remember that fact. Many people have been martyred in the name of Jesus. Others have been driven away from their families because they followed Christ. And still others have sacrificed comforts and money and possessions in the name of Christ.

Full of Grace

Of all the predicaments in which God has placed His people, Mary's virgin conception of Jesus is certainly one that stands out.

Mary was in a tight jam. She was embarking on an impossible journey that would now become a reality. Why? Because God had a plan for humanity—and for Mary; He had really big things in store for her. She would give birth to the Messiah.

But for this to occur in God's will, Mary would walk through the valley of the shadow of death. Her life would be on the line.

Back then, society had rules. There were laws and expectations. There was a line, and Mary would be in a position where all who knew her would assume she had crossed that line. She was on a fast track to being forever outcast from society on account of immorality.

For all they knew, Mary had gone where no one should go, and there was a major threat that she'd be stoned and killed and that anyone suspected to be the father of her unborn child could also be stoned and killed.

Needless to say, this was pretty serious stuff. But Mary's response showed incredible faith.

God's commands don't always match up to society's perceptions, but they always match up with God's will. Always.

The Heart of a Servant

We're going to look at Luke, chapter 1, beginning with

verse 26:

> *In the sixth month of Elizabeth's pregnancy, God sent the angel Gabriel to Nazareth, a town in Galilee, to a virgin pledged to be married to a man named Joseph, a descendant of David. The virgin's name was Mary. The angel went to her and said, "Greetings, you who are highly favored! The Lord is with you."*
>
> *Mary was greatly troubled at his words and wondered what kind of greeting this might be. But the angel said to her, "Do not be afraid, Mary; you have found favor with God. You will conceive and give birth to a son, and you are to call him Jesus. He will be great and will be called the Son of the Most High. The Lord God will give him the throne of his father David, and he will reign over Jacob's descendants forever; his kingdom will never end."*
>
> *"How will this be," Mary asked the angel, "since I am a virgin?"*
>
> *The angel answered, "The Holy Spirit will come on you, and the power of the Most High will overshadow you. So the holy one to be born will be called the Son of God. Even Elizabeth your relative is going to have a child in her old age, and she who was said to be unable to conceive is in her sixth month. For no word from God will ever fail."*
>
> *"I am the Lord's servant," Mary answered. "May your word to me be fulfilled." Then the angel left her.*
> **—Luke 1:26–38**

First, let's put this story in context. At this time, Mary was betrothed, or engaged, to Joseph. Even though they weren't yet married, they were still considered almost as such by the Jewish culture of the day. If the betrothal were to end by either party walking away, it would have been considered a divorce.

You can see, then, that Mary and Joseph's relationship was very serious. They weren't yet married, but they were on a sacred road, walking into a holy covenant together. And, according to Jewish custom, they would walk this path for a year before the marriage would be finalized and consummated.

So, try to imagine Mary. She was in the midst of an engagement and then an angel showed up, telling her that he had good news. His "good news" was that the Holy Spirit was going to come upon her and cause her to conceive and give birth to a child.

And you can just see her confusion. Luke 1:34 says, "'How will this be,' Mary asked the angel, 'since I am a virgin?'"

I'm sure she was thinking, "Can't you wait a year? Why *now?* Do you realize the shame that will come on me? Do you realize my life will be in danger?" She had to be full of questions and probably a bit of concern!

We can just imagine the awkward conversation Mary must have had with Joseph, too. Matthew 1:19 says that Joseph had plans to "divorce her quietly." He wasn't jumping up and down. He wasn't thrilled. He must have assumed right off the bat she had done something wrong. He may have been asking, "With whom has she been sleeping? Anybody I know?" And though the Bible doesn't record it, we can read between the lines that he was upset. He wanted out.

The Bible identifies Joseph as a just man (Matthew 1:19 ESV), or a righteous man (Matthew 1:19 NASB). And even though he had plans to part from Mary, we know that there was nothing in him that wanted to hurt her. He wasn't vengeful. He wasn't punitive in his actions. He simply wanted a quiet, low-key dismissal. In a sense, he was trying to protect them both.

Here was a man who, by all standards of society, had been violated and hurt deeply. And yet his becomes a story of compassion, grace, protection, and care. It is the gospel story unfolding even before Christ showed up.

The angel went to Joseph and confirmed what Mary had told him. He confirmed that Mary was pregnant with a child from the Holy Spirit and that Joseph was going to name him Emmanuel, meaning "God with us."

And Joseph got it. From that point on, he was on board.

So, what did God have in mind here? Why was He bucking the rules of society and even giving the appearance of violating His own commandments on sexual purity? Wouldn't there have been a better way to bring the Messiah into the midst of humanity? What was at stake here?

Choose to Sing

It's common for us to have our lives mapped out the way we want them to go. But usually, we discover that our maps aren't all that smooth. Not everything we hope will happen actually does. We hit bumps along the way, and we get bruises that leave us struggling. Our once-perfect vision for life is muddled.

Typically, when we talk about the perfect life, we talk about acceptance, love, wealth, honor, security. The perfect life is about us more than it is about God. It usually has more to do with our ease than with the needs of others.

So, what's interesting about this Bible story is how God comes in and, from all appearances, snatches the perfect life away from Mary.

This young teenage girl with wonderful dreams of the perfect marriage and a secure future found herself pregnant before the covenant was ever sealed. This wasn't the way she had dreamed of walking down the aisle. This was not in her plan. But she was a godly woman.

In this seemingly absurd and outrageous command to Mary, it appears that God's desire for Mary's perfect life was cast aside. But, in fact, Mary was given a profound and sacred honor—one that would impact all of humanity for all of eternity.

I assure you that, when you sit down with Mary someday, she won't regret the shame others attempted to put upon her.

What appeared as a blot on Mary's character was actually a sign that she was "highly favored" (Luke 1:28). In Luke 1:46–55, Mary sang what we've come to know as the *Magnificat*. In this, she was so honored to have God's favor that she understood it to be a blessing. She saw the good in the struggle. She understood the purpose behind the pain.

And this happened while she was living in a society that viewed her shamefully as a disgrace. Despite that, she sang.

If you were to look at your life right now, and if you were to write a song of praise for a tremendous blessing that you see, what would it be about? Would it be about your kids, your spouse, your job, or maybe some monumental event that's occurred? Maybe you might even sing about your new life? The freedom you've found.

Some might say they can't think of a thing for which to praise God, because it would appear to them that He's absent from their lives and that He doesn't care. They may feel that all they see on the horizon is grief and hurt and a whole lot more coming down the line. Maybe this is you. Maybe you have no joy, peace, or hope.

Do we have the ability to see God's presence, even in what appear to be bad circumstances?

I'm not saying that, just because we walk with God, we are exempt from being pushed to the wall. But what I am saying is that we should strive to respond as Mary did. She saw the good in a strange situation.

Expect the Unexpected

In today's America, we are expected to be more politically correct than truthful. We are discouraged from speaking reality if it offends someone. We are mocked if we speak out against something the Bible speaks out against.

Society determines right and wrong. And in our culture, it is better to not offend someone who ignores God than to offend God Himself. This is the world in which we live.

God's commands don't always match up with society's perceptions, but they always match up with God's will.

Mary faced this head on. She was unmarried, unstained, and extremely vulnerable to the ways of her society, yet she chose God's will. She chose the servant's heart.

You would almost expect God Incarnate to come in with guns blazing—a mighty and powerful army of angels overthrowing governments and throwing evil people out of this world. But, instead, He came in the flesh and blood of a helpless little boy! He came in a way that was viewed by outsiders as shameful and immoral—a birth outside of wedlock. And He did this to reveal that salvation was available to *all* of us.

If you're going to talk about something that really seems bizarre, it's not the pregnancy. (The Lord can make worlds out of His very words, so pregnancy without sexual intercourse is really not that big of a miracle.) What's bizarre and outrageous? The incarnation itself.

A beautiful Advent devotion puts it poignantly: "This absurd contrast and miraculous conjoining—of divine infinity and human finitude, of God's holiness and our sinfulness—is the ultimate religious scandal."[6]

And, in all of it, despite it not being what everyone would have expected, Mary had the strength to trust. She welcomed the absurd and outrageous command with open arms.

Prayer

God, help me to see You in all of my circumstances and to know You are at work. To acknowledge You as my Father and to walk with You for Your glory.

Father, this is one of those stories that is so riveting. I've heard it many times, yet I feel I've barely scratched the surface. Help me to have Mary's heart. Help me to be open to You even when it puts me in a difficult situation.

You are my Father. And You desire that Your will be enacted in my life in the same manner that it was in Joseph's and Mary's lives. It doesn't matter how society perceives it. It's whether or not You will it.

I pray this in the name of our Lord and Savior, Jesus Christ. Amen.

WORKBOOK

Chapter Six Questions

Question: How were Mary and Joseph "in a jam"? Describe a time when you felt God put you in a difficult situation.

_____

_____

_____

_____

_____

_____

_____

_____

_____

_____

_____

_____

Question: Are you willing to suffer shame and disgrace for the sake of the gospel? How might that manifest itself in the current culture in which you live?

_____

_____

_____

_____

_____

_____

_____

_____

_____

_____

_____

Question: Read Mary's song found in Luke 1:46–55. What did her choice to sing (and what do the words of her song) reveal about her heart?

_____

_____

_____

_____

_____

_____

_____

_____

_____

_____

_____

_____

Action: Describe your own vision of your perfect life. Then describe God's vision for you as best as you can, based on the teachings of Scripture and the leading of the Holy Spirit. Where are the visions similar, and where are they dissimilar? Whose plan will you follow? Write out a song or prayer of praise for the life God has given you and the callings He has entrusted to you.

_____

_____

_____

_____

_____

_____

_____

_____

_____

_____

Chapter Six Notes

_____

_____

_____

_____

_____

_____

_____

_____

_____

_____

_____

_____

_____

_____

_____

_____

_____

_____

_____

_____

_____

_____

CHAPTER SEVEN

Walk on Water!

"Lord, if it's you," Peter replied, "tell me to come to you on the water." "Come," he said. Then Peter got down out of the boat, walked on the water and came toward Jesus.
—Matthew 14:28–29

You might have heard the expression "Out of the frying pan and into the fire." The idea is that there are times when the moment we get out of one bad situation, we find ourselves in the middle of another!

Many books and movies feature these kinds of situations. Just when the hero is about to save the day, he realizes that there is much more going on than he thought.

I think of the television show *American Ninja Warrior*. Competitors must face one obstacle after another, each getting harder and harder as their muscles get weaker and weaker. I imagine that, somewhere in the middle of the obstacle course, it's common for new athletes to wonder, "What have I gotten myself into?"

Veteran athletes, on the other hand, know that in just a

few more obstacles, they'll reach their goal.

As Christians, we've all been in situations where it seems as if God is asking us to do much more than we anticipated. He is pushing us further outside the bounds of what we would consider normal, realistic, or even plausible. And what happens? We quickly dismiss His call.

Absurd Meets Outrageous

Immediately Jesus made the disciples get into the boat and go on ahead of him to the other side while dismissed he the crowd. After he had dismissed them, he went up on a mountainside by himself to pray. Later that night, he was there alone, and the boat was already a considerable distance from land, buffeted by the waves because the wind was against it.

Shortly before dawn Jesus went out to them walking on the lake. When the disciples saw him walking on the lake they were terrified. "It's a ghost," they said and cried out in fear.

But Jesus immediately said to them, "Take courage. It is I. Don't be afraid."

"Lord, if it's you," Peter replied, "tell me to come to you on the water."

"Come," he said.

Then Peter got down out of the boat, walked on the water and came toward Jesus. But when he saw the wind he was afraid and beginning to sink cried out, "Lord, save me."

Immediately Jesus reached out his hand and caught him. "You of little faith," he said, "Why did you doubt?"

And when they climbed into the boat the wind died down. And those who were in the boat worshiped him saying,

"Truly, you are the Son of God."
—Matthew 14:22–32

In Mathew 14, Peter and the disciples found themselves on the Sea of Galilee in very troubled waters. Suddenly Jesus appeared on the water. Peter, man of moxie that he was, challenged the identity of Jesus. He gave Christ an absurd command, and Jesus responded with an equally outrageous response.

Peter said, "Tell me to come to You." And Jesus said, "Come."

This was unprecedented! The danger was overwhelming, and certain death was the consequence of this kind of action, because of the severity of the storm upon the waters.

But Jesus was involved.

We become so familiar sometimes with Bible stories that we don't realize how outside the norm some of these events really were. And while we sometimes position ourselves like, "Oh yeah, I would do what Peter did," I bet most of us wouldn't. I don't think I would have jumped out of the boat. I don't think I would have been like these courageous figures we read about in the Scriptures—although we like to identify ourselves with them.

As we look at this particular passage in the context of faith, we see that faith will take us to, and *through*, the most dangerous of circumstances, as long as we never take our focus off of Christ.

A Sea of Storms

It is important to remember what was going on prior to this event. In Matthew 14:1–12, we learn that Herod killed John the Baptist. Word was then brought to Christ, and no doubt there was a lot of discussion and grieving among Jesus and His disciples. Following that, we read of the miracle of the feeding of the five thousand (Matthew 14:13–21).

So, imagine grieving over John the Baptist, then being followed by a huge multitude of people, and finally witnessing Jesus singlehandedly create food to feed them all.

The emotional spectrum that surrounded Jesus and His disciples was enormous. From grief to ecstasy to wonder to worship.

Where the above passage picks up, Jesus had sent His disciples out on a boat on the Sea of Galilee to cross to the other side. The Scriptures tell us that Jesus needed some one-on-one time with His Father (Matthew 14:13).

Now, if I could take you to the Sea of Galilee, which is literally a lake, you would see that it's sitting roughly 650 feet below sea level. It continues to follow the Jordan River down to where it dumps out in the Dead Sea, which is about 1,350 feet below sea level.

The Sea of Galilee is surrounded by a mountain range. And because of the topography around the Sea of Galilee, storms can sweep in very quickly. The meteorological conditions, the mountains, everything together make it such that storms can hit the sea just like that. And, as the disciples found out, if you're out there when a storm hits, you're in trouble.

Before they knew it, the disciples were surrounded by strong winds and high waves. Meanwhile, Jesus was on His way out to meet them. His mode of transportation? Walking on water. Clearly out of the ordinary, but we have to remember that He had been praying to the Father. He had been alone with God, thinking about everything that had unfolded, from the death of John the Baptist to the feeding of the five thousand to the power of God at work and the cost involved. It makes sense that the presence of God would have an impact.

And what happened when the disciples saw Him coming? Peter asked to join in.

More Than Just Positive Thinking

Can you imagine what might have happened if Peter had asked the other disciples whether or not he should attempt to walk on the water? Good grief! I'm sure they would have emphatically said, "Stay in the boat!" Only an idiot would jump out into the water under the conditions they were in.

I'm not sure why life is this way, but there are far more people who say *don't* and *can't* than there are ones who say *do* and *can*. And I'm not talking about "positive thinking." I'm talking about real, true faith. There is a vast difference.

Positive thinking says, "I can do whatever I think I can do." Faith says, "I can do whatever God calls me to do." That's a big, big difference. Yet I'm surprised at the number of Christians, people who say they believe in God's power and in Christ, who have no faith that God can do what He has asked His people to do. And because they don't believe, because they don't have the faith, they tend to say *no, can't, don't.*

I know I'm superimposing this on the disciples, and I'm doing so based on their responses along the road. When Peter said to them, "Hey, I'm going out there to Jesus," he didn't ask their permission—but can you imagine if he had? How many of those disciples would have told him to go for it? How many would have told him to stay in the boat?

I'm guessing the other disciples were the "Cold Water Committee." The disciples were the ones sitting back, going, "Are you nuts? What's your health insurance like? Have you made funeral arrangements? Hey, we're not coming in after you when you start going under!" I could see them acting like Peter was an idiot, because let's face it: stepping out on the water was an absurd, outrageous thing to do!

And I'm not just pointing fingers, either, because I'm certain that, if I had been in the boat and he'd asked *me,* I would have done some *can't, don't, no* talk of my own. I might have said, "Peter, have you prayed about this? What great theological substance or truth is going to emerge from you walking out to Jesus on the water?"

But for him to get in the water and walk out there was so daring. It was so out of the box. This is something that you just don't do. It was unprecedented. It was absurd and outrageous.

Seek Out Encouragers

One mistake we often make is seeking counsel from the wrong places. If you're attempting the impossible, many people will tell you why you can't do it. They will freely offer advice against your plan.

Don't take their advice to heart. Don't get counsel from those who will discourage you.

Almost everyone has had other people make assertions about what he or she can't do. And if you haven't had many people try to explain why this or that won't work, then I bet you've done plenty of that negative talk on your own.

You've probably said, "You want me to do *what?* I can't, God. I don't have those abilities. I don't have that skill. I don't have the right kind of boldness. I'm not articulate. I can't, I don't, I won't...." Our language is full of this negativity, and negative self-talk is the worst of all.

This is why seeking out those who will encourage you to step out in your faith is so crucial to living the life you are called to live. Find spiritual people and get their advice. Soak it in. Then, if you believe God is calling you to do something great, your community will boost you and help you to follow that outrageous command.

Keep Your Focus

When Peter stepped out of the boat, he started to walk on the water. Scripture makes that very clear. And whenever we talk about this part of the story, we talk about how and why he began to sink.

It wasn't that he was looking at the waves crashing around him. Rather, the scripture says, he started looking at the wind—the wind that created the waves. In other words, *he shifted his attention from the One who ruled the waters to what he thought ruled the waters.*

When we start looking at other people or circumstances, we lose focus. We agree that the absurd, outrageous command is exactly that—crazy. When we start looking at all the things taking place around us, we lose focus. And when we lose focus, we start to sink.

We don't need to be driven by the wind. We need to be tied to the anchor. We need to be so riveted on Christ that, regardless of what comes before us, we can see through it because we see the big picture.

Phillips Brooks said the Bible is like a telescope. If you look *through* a telescope, you can see incredible things—stars and planets and beauty beyond imagination. But if you look *at* a telescope, all you will see is a telescope.[7]

If we look through the eyes of Christ, if we look through the Word, He opens up to us incredible insights and wisdom. But if we just look at the Bible without engaging Christ, then all we see is a book. All we see are words, and we miss the opportunity to go beyond them.

Expect Jesus to Be There

I remember doing a children's sermon where I wanted to demonstrate the difference in our lives when we are filled with the Spirit. I was using a glove and was going to show the children the difference in the glove being empty as opposed to having a hand fill it. I laid the glove on the altar and asked the kids to give it a command. One of the boys said, "Lie there!" It wasn't what I was expecting!

I think we would like God to give us the "Lie there. Stay there. Do nothing" type of commands. But instead, God wants us to get out of the boat, to start walking, and to get out of our comfort zones.

There are many things that keep us firm and fast and not wanting to move. However, movement is exactly what God wants.

There is another example in Scripture of Peter leaping out of the boat and running to Jesus. Now, in that instance, he didn't walk on the water, but it was meaningful nonetheless.

In John 21, Jesus Christ had been crucified and resurrected. Peter, meanwhile, had betrayed Him. He had denied Christ three times, and he was incredibly ashamed of this (John 18:25–27).

In the passage, Peter and some of the disciples were out fishing without much success. But Jesus showed up on the shore. When Peter recognzied Jesus, what did he do? He jumped out of the boat to get to the shore (John 21:7)!

In this story, Peter was hurting, and, more than anything, else he longed for the Lord to give him relief. He had confidence that, when he jumped out of that boat and headed for the Lord, everything would be all right.

I think God is sometimes frustrated with us because He has given us opportunity after opportunity to get out of the boat and walk on water, or to get out of the boat and join Him, and we've said "no." And it's *because* we've said "no" that we live our lives without any confidence in what

God can do.

Great opportunities arise—absurd, outrageous ones—and God says, "Do this."

We say, "But how do I know I'll be okay? I've never trusted You before—why start now?"

If we keep our focus on the Lord and get out of the boat, we will discover that He is able to do far more than we could ever imagine.

Sometimes, when we set out to serve and follow the Lord, our minds and hearts get distracted. We look around and fall in love with things that don't matter, and we neglect what does matter. We become fearful in our service. We think we can't do what God is asking us to do—and our conviction about who Christ is wanes.

Trying to accomplish the impossible can never happen unless we move forward by faith and get out of our comfort zones.

Even when we feel like we are sinking, God is still there. All we need to do is move toward Him. Have confidence that He is going to grab us if needed. When we accept and understand and *believe* this, then our confidence in Him flourishes. Our faith is bolstered. We no longer shy away from the things He asks us to do.

But how can we know if we don't ever get out of the boat?

I love being on the water—boating, swimming, water skiing. One time our family borrowed a friend's boat to go out on the lake. I remember backing up to put the trailer down to the water, then releasing the boat with all the family piled inside. Then I pulled the truck back out and parked it.

I got in the boat and started to back into the lake when I noticed we were rapidly taking on water. I started to panic, worried about sinking someone else's boat. We couldn't bail fast enough, and I couldn't figure out what the problem was. So, we headed back. I jumped out and got the truck backed up to trailer it in. We managed to pull the boat out of the water before it sank.

I watched the water drain out of it, waiting to see what had caused the problem.

If you know anything about boats, you'll know there's a plug in the back that needs to be inserted in order for the boat to float. Well, it was unplugged. And I hadn't even bothered to check it before getting in the water.

I think part of our dilemma is that we have holes in our thinking and in our dreams. These holes let bad advice seep in and Christ's promises seep out. These holes have been created by doubt, past failure, fears, and other people.

But we can't plug them back up with pep talks and positive thinking. We can only plug them up with faith and trust that what God has called us to do is backed by the power of the Holy Spirit.

What holes need to be plugged up so that you can walk on water? What are you focused on that is allowing your dreams to take on water and go under?

Don't become a prisoner to your fears. Don't let a fear of failure keep you tied to the dock or clinging to the side of the boat. Don't let the absurd outrageous deter you. Amazing things await you on the other side.

Get out of the boat and walk. He will be there to catch you if you fall.

Prayer

Father, You've asked me to share my faith, to let my light shine, and to walk with You boldly, unapologetically. In all of these commands, help me to remember that You're with me. Help me to respond to You in faith.

Thank You for the boldness You provide. Thank You for giving us Your Spirit. It is by faith that I will get out of the boat and walk on water.

May Your name be praised, in Christ's name. Amen.

WORKBOOK

Chapter Seven Questions

Question: What are some ways in which people gather opinions about following Jesus instead of getting out of the boat? Who in your life offers you encouragement to walk in faith? When others seek your advice, do you tell them to play it safe, or to boldly trust the Lord?

_____

_____

_____

_____

_____

_____

_____

_____

_____

_____

_____

Question: What is the difference between faith and positive thinking? Which one do you see embraced more often, and why do you think that is? Which one guides your own life?

_____

_____

_____

_____

_____

_____

_____

_____

_____

_____

_____

Question: What are some of the "winds of life" that cause you to lose focus on Christ? How can you keep your attention on Him instead of circumstances?

_____

_____

_____

_____

_____

_____

_____

_____

_____

_____

_____

Action: Write down a list of holes in your thinking (brought on by doubt, failures, fears, or people) that are hindering you from experiencing all that God has for you. Next to each hole, write a truth from Scripture that will encourage and guide you.

Chapter Seven Notes

_____

_____

_____

_____

_____

_____

_____

_____

_____

_____

_____

_____

_____

_____

_____

_____

_____

_____

_____

_____

_____

_____

CHAPTER NINE

Feed the People!

Jesus then took the loaves, gave thanks, and distributed to those who were seated as much as they wanted. He did the same with the fish.

—John 6:11

Do you ever compare yourself with others? It's easy in this day and age to spend time online and come away feeling as though we have nothing to offer. Everyone else seems so successful, happy, good looking, and healthy. Everyone seems to have what it takes.

We bring this mindset to our spiritual lives, too. "He's a great speaker." "She really knows her Bible." "He is so much gentler with people than I am." "She really knows how to strike up a conversation about God."

But what if I told you that what you have today, right now, at this very moment, is enough?

The story of Jesus feeding the five thousand is an incredible example of something small being exactly what God needed.

It's also a great example of an absurd, outrageous command.

"Feed My People"

When Jesus asked his disciples about feeding the multitude, they had to have thought that the request was extreme. Where would they get the food? How could they possibly afford it? Wouldn't it take all day?

I can imagine that they would have been more understanding if the command were to heal people, or teach, or love people. But feed them? A crowd of five thousand men, plus women and children?

They certainly must have been feeling as though they wouldn't be able to come up with a solution. But Jesus was about to show how He can take a little and turn it into a lot.

Let's look at John's gospel, beginning with verse one, of chapter six.

Some time after this, Jesus crossed to the far shore of the Sea of Galilee (that is, the Sea of Tiberias), and a great crowd of people followed him because they saw the signs he had performed by healing the sick. Then Jesus went up on a mountainside and sat down with his disciples. The Jewish Passover Festival was near.

When Jesus looked up and saw a great crowd coming toward him, he said to Philip, "Where shall we buy bread for these people to eat?" He asked this only to test him, for he already had in mind what he was going to do.

Philip answered him, "It would take more than half a year's wages to buy enough bread for each one to have a bite!"

Another of his disciples, Andrew, Simon Peter's brother, spoke up, "Here is a boy with five small barley loaves and two small fish, but how far will they go among so many?"

Jesus said, "Have the people sit down." There was plenty of grass in that place, and they sat down (about five thousand men were there). Jesus then took the loaves, gave thanks, and distributed to those who were seated as much as they wanted. He did the same with the fish.

When they had all had enough to eat, he said to his disciples, "Gather the pieces that are left over. Let nothing be wasted." So they gathered them and filled twelve baskets with the pieces of the five barley loaves left over by those who had eaten.

After the people saw the sign Jesus performed, they began to say, "Surely this is the Prophet who is to come into the world." Jesus, knowing that they intended to come and make him king by force, withdrew again to a mountain by himself.

—John 6:1–15

Let me set up the story, so that we get a better understanding of just how bizarre this whole miracle was.

The scripture notes they were in the Passover season. This is significant because it helps to understand what kind of bread this little boy brought for his lunch. It was not like your nice sourdough or yeast bread; Passover bread was unleavened, flat crackers.

Not only was the bread nothing special, his fish wasn't salmon, or tuna, or anything fancy. People ate salted, dried fish in those days—most likely sardines.

The text says the boy had five barley loaves and two fish, but to help the significance of this miracle stick in your mind, I want you to imagine the barley loaves and fish have been put together. Essentially, the boy had a sardine sandwich in his lunch box that he offered to Jesus.

I've often wondered what it must've been like to be the little boy in this passage. He took enough food to last awhile and set out for a normal day, completely unaware of how his life would be forever changed. At some point in the day—maybe he had planned it, maybe not—he began following Jesus. He was part of the "uncounted" crowd of followers. That is, since he was not a man yet, he was not among the five thousand men who were counted. Neither was his mother, who probably made his lunch.

Intrigued, the young boy listened to Jesus preach. He became enthralled with His teachings about the Kingdom of God and love and forgiveness, and he ended up spending the whole day listening and learning.

And then he was part of a miracle.

You've Got What It Takes

The resources for a miracle are always present—our challenge is to not overlook them.

In the time of Christ, meals were used for reconciliation. Jesus not only wanted to feed the crowd physically, He wanted to transform them spiritually by communicating the importance of reconciliation to the people.

And everything He needed to achieve what He wanted to achieve was present. Just five loaves and two fish. Sure, it seems lean when you're staring into the faces of thousands of people, but remember, God's business is multiplication. Satan's business is division.

It's easy to look at this particular story, this miracle, and think, what if the boy had not brought his lunch?

God would have worked it out. He would have found something else.

Please don't miss this: everything that God needs to do wonders and miracles in your life and to make you effective for Him is already present. You don't have to go searching for the right personality trait or words to say. He will work with what you already have. He will multiply whatever you put in His hands. Even sardine sandwiches.

That little boy had very little to offer, but out of what he had, Jesus found the building materials for a miracle.

There's no indication anybody else had brought food with them. Or maybe they did, and maybe this little boy was the only one willing to surrender his lunch. If you think about that, maybe a little boy was the only one that didn't doubt that his lunch would feed the massive crowd.

A critical truth in the Christian life is that Jesus uses what we bring. We may not have much to bring Him according to the world's standards, or even according our own, but He uses what we have. Sometimes that seems simply absurd, but it's true.

And what if the world is denied miracle after miracle simply because we will not bring to Christ what we have and who we are? How many lives have not been touched because we refused to speak? How many needs have not been met because we weren't obedient?

Miracles can still happen. Wonders are possible. But when we don't offer up what we have, then we stop those things before they even get going.

Nothing Wasted

When you place your gifts in God's hands, you can expect something wonderful. When you give God your barley loaves and sardines, you can expect something wonderful. When you give God your pain, you can expect something wonderful.

And when you place yourself in God's hands, you can most certainly expect incredible things to happen.

Just as He told His disciples to gather the leftovers, He will take what you give Him and use every last bit. Nothing will go to waste. Nothing will be tossed aside or forgotten.

It's easy to think that we can do a lot more with what we've got than God can. But in Malachi 3:10, God says, "'Test me in this,' says the Lord Almighty, 'and see if I will not throw open the floodgates of heaven and pour out so much blessing that there will not be room enough to store.'"

We can serve wholeheartedly and still have more left over if Christ is in it. God really does deal in the immeasurably more. What we consider to be absurd and outrageous, He considers to be the norm.

Are you holding back from God while at the same time looking for immeasurably more? Are you blocking Him, holding on to your loaves and fishes, yet still expecting Him to come through?

Several years ago, God asked me to do a forty-day fast. I thought, "You've got to be kidding!" Talk about absurd. It took me a year and a half before I finally consented to be obedient. At the time, I was traveling and speaking around the country and found myself at a lot of banquets. But the Lord helped me according to His immeasurably more abundant ways.

During the last week of the fast, I wanted to go to my office but discovered that our van had a flat tire. I changed the tire, but afterward I was exhausted. Good grief!

Then I thought, "Well, I haven't eaten in a few weeks, so I guess there's not much gas in the tank."

When I went to pray at lunchtime, God spoke clearly to me: "Tom, if I hadn't sustained you, this is how you would have felt for the entire fast."

Wow! I got the message. And then, after prayer, I was fine through the end of the fast.

It seemed absurd to do a forty-day fast. But had I disobeyed, I wouldn't have come to understand the sustaining grace of God. He multiplied my strength without me taking in anything physically to make it happen.

Let Him Multiply

Many of the people that day must have eaten what they were given without thinking much about it—without realizing the miracle that had gone on. There was no sound system to announce what was happening. There was no Twitter or Facebook.

All this food was being passed around and people were eating until they were stuffed, and they may have thought, "Wow, that's so nice of them for feeding us. I wonder where they got all this food?"

But there was a small group that knew exactly what had occurred and how phenomenal the miracle was. And those people told the story. They wrote it down. They made sure it was remembered, and we're still reading about it today.

I wonder how many battles we face because we never extend ourselves beyond ourselves? We never put ourselves in a position where we would trust the Lord. We just sit around, waiting for the basket to come our way, content to be oblivious.

What is God asking you to give? I'm not just talking

about money here. What's God asking of you? Your talents and your skills? Your insights? Your intellect?

God says, "Give me what you've got and let me multiply it."

He's asking us to make a difference in the world. But He doesn't want us doing it in our own strength. He's asking us to give over what we have, to let Him multiply it. The result could be a story for the ages.

Prayer

Father, I thank you that this story of multiplication is more than a story, it's a reality. I pray you would help me to get beyond myself. I pray that I would give you all of who I am and all I have.

I ask that You multiply my influence for You and multiply anything I have for You.

Lord, thank You for your goodness. May Your name be praised in Christ's most holy name. Amen.

WORKBOOK

Chapter Nine Questions

Question: Are you constantly comparing yourself to other people? In your spiritual life, are you tempted to think that, unlike others, you don't have enough to offer to make a difference? How do these comparisons make you feel? What is the antidote to this kind of thinking?

_____

_____

_____

_____

_____

_____

_____

_____

_____

_____

_____

Question: Do you remember a time when you thought you had too little to offer to God, but were obedient in handing it over to Him, and He abundantly blessed the little you had?

_____

_____

_____

_____

_____

_____

_____

_____

_____

_____

_____

Question: The little boy with the loaves and fish may have been the only person in the crowd that day who had faith that his small lunch could feed everyone. Can you think of an opportunity you missed, or something you've withheld from God, because you did not show this kind of faith in His ability to use small things and flawed people?

Can you imagine what God might have done if you had responded in faith and said "yes" in that situation? How will you respond next time?

_____

_____

_____

_____

_____

_____

_____

_____

_____

_____

Action: Remember that everything God needs to work miracles in your life is already present. What is God asking you to give to Him so He can multiply it for the good of others? Make a list of "small things" that you think God is asking you to hand over to Him. Begin praying for these areas, and make a commitment to follow God's leading— even if what you have to offer seems insignificant in your own eyes. Keep track of what God does with your "loaves and fish."

Chapter Notes

_____

_____

_____

_____

_____

_____

_____

_____

_____

_____

_____

_____

_____

_____

_____

_____

_____

_____

_____

_____

_____

_____

_____

_____

CHAPTER NINE

Forgive Others!

While they were stoning him, Stephen prayed, "Lord Jesus, receive my spirit." Then he fell on his knees and cried out, "Lord, do not hold this sin against them." When he had said this, he fell asleep.

—Acts 7:59-60

In the midst of his own death at the hands of his fellow Jews—for the "sin" of speaking gospel truth—Stephen, the church's first martyr, followed beautifully in the steps of his Savior, saying, "Father, forgive them."

Can we fathom such a selfless act? As if dying for sharing the gospel truth wasn't enough, as if dying at the hands of those who had called you brother and who sincerely believed killing you was an act of obedience to God wasn't enough, as if the enormous pain of being *stoned to death* wasn't sufficient to get you into the Martyrs' Hall of Fame (if such a thing existed)—on top of it all, Stephen prayed for forgiveness for his very murderers.

Friends, if this isn't an example of a Christian following an absurd, outrageous command of God, nothing is. "Love your enemies" and "pray for those who persecute you" (Matthew 5:44) are outlandish directives.

How do we do it? How can we follow the example of Stephen, who was following the example of Jesus, who prayed for the forgiveness for His murderers, too, from the very cross?

Let's acknowledge some things first. For starters, we've all been hurt. And we've all hurt others. Second, forgiveness isn't easy. Forgiveness is hard, especially in long-term relationships. It costs something to forgive. Third, forgiveness is often confused with ignoring the offense.

So, will we forgive? *Can* we forgive? What does forgiveness really mean and not mean? How do we do it?

When we are hurt and wounded by others, why would we want to forgive them? You know what it's like to be at odds with people. We've all been there. Relational viruses attack every friendship. Tensions arise. Wrongs are done. Lies are told. Trust is broken.

Because we're imperfect people, we're bound to have trouble with forgiveness and the giving of grace. I'm convinced that relationships are built not on a standard of perfection, but on our ability to ask for forgiveness, and upon our willingness to extend forgiveness to other people. In other words, grace must impact both our friendships and our forgiveness. Grace is more than a prayer offered before a meal; grace is the glue that holds people together. There is no relationship of any kind—

marriage, friendship, work, or family—that will last without the grace of forgiveness at work.

If you and I want to have relationships that last for the long haul, then we must be willing to extend forgiveness to others. There are at least two reasons why we struggle with forgiveness: Forgiveness is not natural, and forgiveness is not fair—our sense of justice wants to be vindicated.

This is where Jesus takes us far beyond anything offered in this world. He ushers us into a world of grace that is desperately needed and wanted by all who live.

Then Peter came to Jesus and asked, "Lord, how many times shall I forgive my brother or sister who sins against me? Up to seven times?"

Jesus answered, "I tell you, not seven times, but seventy-seven times.

"Therefore, the kingdom of heaven is like a king who wanted to settle accounts with his servants. As he began the settlement, a man who owed him ten thousand bags of gold was brought to him. Since he was not able to pay, the master ordered that he and his wife and his children and all that he had be sold to repay the debt.

"At this the servant fell on his knees before him. 'Be patient with me,' he begged, 'and I will pay back everything.' The servant's master took pity on him, canceled the debt and let him go.

"But when that servant went out, he found one of his fellow servants who owed him a hundred silver coins. He grabbed him and began to choke him. 'Pay back what you owe me!' he demanded.

"His fellow servant fell to his knees and begged him, 'Be patient with me, and I will pay it back.'

"But he refused. Instead, he went off and had the man thrown into prison until he could pay the debt. When the other servants saw what had happened, they were outraged and went and told their master everything that had happened.

"Then the master called the servant in. 'You wicked servant,' he said, 'I canceled all that debt of yours because you begged me to. Shouldn't you have had mercy on your fellow servant just as I had on you?' In anger his master handed him over to the jailers to be tortured, until he should pay back all he owed.

"This is how my heavenly Father will treat each of you unless you forgive your brother or sister from your heart."
—Matthew 18:21–35

When His disciples asked how many times they needed to forgive another person, thinking two or three might be the limit, or even as many as seven times, Jesus said: *Seventy times seven.* Yikes—that's absurd!

Jesus Is Our Example

Forgiveness is not the norm. In fact, it's so far outside the norm that, when we hear stories of forgiveness, we are actually amazed and moved. Our enemy, Satan, encourages us to hurt one another over and over again. When the pain has been inflicted, he then sits on the sore and tender spots of the wounds, telling us we should seek revenge. He makes us think that bitterness and grudges are worth carrying, because the offender needs to pay. And who better to avenge than the one carrying an unforgiving spirit, a spirit that leaves the person owning it in shambles along the side of the road, left for dead?

We must realize that Satan is at war with us, and unforgiveness isn't simply a difficult emotion; it is a deadly virus. It infects all we think and do. The enemy doesn't inject us with truth serum; he infects us with self-righteousness that leads to unforgiveness.

It seems absurd that Jesus would forgive our sins and transform us. Absurd that He would engage us wherever we are and in whatever condition we are living. He desires always to make us new creations. That's why, on the cross, instead of calling out the angels to bring Him down from the cross and take revenge on those who crucified Him, He sought forgiveness for them and us in His most gut-wrenching hour (Luke 23:34).

Our rules of engagement for addressing unforgiveness seem to miss the point. We want to assess the motives of the person who hurt us. We look at the severity of the scar inflicted by the assault. We put ourselves in a position of needing to dole out justice for the one who was victimized. And we tend to put conditions on the substance of the forgiveness we may offer.

We say things like, "Okay, I'll let it go this once, but it had better never happen again!" In other words, "I have a limited supply of forgiveness and if I use it for you, I'm out." In no way does that reflect the person of Christ.

Or we say, "I'll forgive, but I won't forget." In other words, "Don't cross me again. I'm going to hang on to this sin of yours in case I need to throw it back in your face."

Why would Christ tell us to forgive over and over again? It seems absurd! The person who hurt us gets off scot-free while we attend to our wounds. He doesn't have to pay for his wrong. But in thinking like that, we miss the point.

The wound is like a festering boil on our skin. It builds up poisonous fluid until something is done about it. So, we lance the wound. But then it builds up fluid again. Should we say, "No more lancing! I did it once!"? Absolutely not! We lance it again, because we don't want the poison in our system.

That's why we forgive over and over: we don't want the poison of unforgiveness in our systems. And, in the bigger picture; when we make a practice of forgiveness, we become more like Christ.

Sometimes, we want the person who hurt us to be punished, but what we need is to be healed.

Key Steps in the Process of Forgiveness

The process of forgiveness involves six key steps:

Acknowledge the Offense

Forgiveness doesn't mean we ignore or overlook the offense. On the contrary! In fact, if we fail to acknowledge the offense, there is nothing to forgive. Or so we pretend. Acknowledgement may bring a sense of pain and grief with it. But that is good, because it validates the offense and the need to forgive. Satan would prefer that we ignore it, so that it can fester and become even more poisonous in our minds. Acknowledge the offense. It doesn't mean you are positioning yourself to attack; it means you are preparing to forgive.

Address Emotional Responses

When we are hurt, our defenses and emotions rise to the occasion and sometimes steer us in the wrong direction. We'll experience such emotions as denial, anger, vengeance, disappointment, grief, self-righteousness, feeling like a victim, and many more. It is natural to become defensive and accusatory when we are hurt, but that brings little satisfaction and offers nothing in the way of healing or godly behavior. Sometimes, the pain is great and requires a great deal of forgiveness to overcome it. Allow yourself the freedom to hurt and grieve, but be sure to keep surrendering these emotions to Christ. They will surface, but they don't have to dictate your responses. Let Christ do that. Unless we forgive, we will never be whole and we ourselves will not be forgiven (Matthew 6:14,15).

Practice Godly Responses

This means we *decide* to forgive. It is important to understand what is happening. More than likely, the person who hurt you suffers from a multitude of hurts. As the old saying goes, "Hurt people hurt people." If you lash out, you are only inflicting more wounds. The person needs Christ, not to be clubbed. If I refuse to forgive someone for his or her wrong action toward me, what I'm doing is holding on to the sin and letting go of the person. When Christ forgives us, He holds on to us and lets our sin go. That is godliness. *A godly response is when we value the offender more than the sin.* We need the help of God to get to this point. We need to surrender the offense to Him and ask Him to give us love for the other person.

Pay the Cost of Forgiveness

As noted in practicing godly responses, we must value the offender more than the sin of the offender. But there is a cost to that: we pay the consequences for the offender's sin. We are left wounded, and the other person may seem unscathed by the incident. Remember, Jesus forgave our sins by dying on the cross for us. He paid the consequences for our sinful actions. In order for us to forgive, we, too, must pay the consequences for the actions of those who've hurt us. That means we may suffer for what they did wrong and we need to pray that God will help them come to grips with their sin so that they can repent.

Experience Freedom

When we forgive, we are freed from the chains of hate and unforgiveness. We are not weighed down by the offenses of others. We are free to love, free to trust, free to be vulnerable, and free to live. Healing occurs in the act of forgiving. Without it, we are poisoned and lost. Remember, we are all guilty of hurting others. We need forgiveness as much or more than we need to extend it. Jesus said that, unless we forgive others, we will not be forgiven (Matthew 6:14–15). Freedom lies in the practice of forgiveness.

Take Ongoing Action

Because we forgive doesn't mean that all of our negative emotions walk out the door. They may resurface multiple times, and Satan will ride them like a Pony Express rider on his way to deliver the mail. Only, his desire will be to deliver you to hell. Forgiveness is a choice, and it must be practiced, sometimes daily. When the emotions resurface and hit us again like a tidal wave, we must resurrender them to Christ. We made the decision to forgive, and our emotions will not dictate our taking ungodly actions.

Real forgiveness leaves the sins of others and our hurts at the feet of Jesus, which helps us leave them in the past. Jesus understands the difficulty of such forgiveness and demonstrated its cost on the cross. Stephen followed Jesus' absurd, outrageous example—at great cost. I pray that all of us can forgive and find freedom in life. To keep on forgiving is a God-like characteristic.

Prayer

God, forgiveness is hard. You know this better than me. You are the One who is completely holy, completely righteous. All sin is ultimately against You. Yet You forgave us even while we were yet sinners (Romans 5:8). You forgive us daily. Help me to be like You. Help me to live in Your forgiveness, and to offer it freely, generously, to others, the way You have offered it to me. Help me be honest and intentional in my acts of forgiveness. And let me live in the freedom and peace that forgiveness affords. In Jesus' name, amen.

Chapter Nine Questions

Question: What is a moving story of forgiveness that you have heard? Why are these stories so amazing?

_____

_____

_____

_____

_____

_____

_____

_____

_____

_____

_____

Question: Have you ever qualified your forgiveness or offered conditional forgiveness? What did that look like? How does conditional forgiveness fall short of Christ's forgiveness for you?

_____

_____

_____

_____

_____

_____

_____

_____

_____

_____

Question: What does it mean to value the offender more than the sin? Other than the cross, what are some examples of Jesus doing this?

_____

_____

_____

_____

_____

_____

_____

_____

_____

_____

_____

_____

Action: Think of a situation in your life that requires on-going forgiveness. What is something you could do to bless your offender? Plan how you will proactively show your forgiveness through a kind deed.

Chapter Nine Notes

CONCLUSION

Say *Yes*!

What is God calling you to do? What absurd, outrageous command are you facing today?

My grandfather was one of my heroes. He gave his life to Christ later in life and then did some pastoring.

Grandpap suffered from rheumatoid arthritis. He was doubled over and paralyzed in that position. Mobility was a challenge. However, he had a great burden for his three boys and one daughter. At night, he would climb the steps, which for us would take a few seconds. For him, it was a two-hour ordeal. Nonetheless, he did it day after day so he could pray over his kids at night.

This seems absurd and outrageous. He could have prayed from downstairs. But God honored his passion. Two of the boys became pastors. His daughter traveled with her husband in music ministry. Counting my grandfather, there are currently four generations of pastors in our family. That's what happens when we answer His call to do the absurd.

Is He calling you to quit your job and take one that pays

less? Give away your comfort? Tell a friend about Christ? Does He want you to step out on faith? Live more for Him? Be the Christian you know you can be?

Each and every day, God has plans for us. He has places He wants to take us and blessings ready to be bestowed on us. And, each and every day, we make choices.

We choose to give it all to Him or to keep a bit for ourselves.

We commit to going all the way, or we drop out partway through our task.

We determine that God is trustworthy and, therefore, His commands are not only feasible, but they're for our benefit. Or, conversely, we decide we're too nervous to trust. We're too afraid of what might happen.

Every day, we make a choice. And every day, God calls us.

Won't you make today the day you say *yes* to His absurd, outrageous commands?

He has big things waiting for those who dare to follow Him—for those who build arks and march around cities and give birth to our Lord.

Don't you want to see what He has planned for you?

Say *yes*! Become one of the followers of the absurd and outrageous.

REFERENCES

Notes

1. West, Grace. "LEGO My Gun: S. I. Boy Faces Suspension Over Tiny Toy Weapon." *NBC 4 New York.* NBC Universal. February 3, 2010. https://www.nbcnewyork.com/news/local/Boy-Threatened-With-Suspension-Over-Toy-Gun-83473992.html.

2. Voskamp, Ann. *One Thousand Gifts.* Zondervan, 2011.

3. "Ancient Jericho: Tell es-Sultan." *United Nations Educational, Scientific, and Cultural Organization.* http://whc.unesco.org/en/tentativelists/5704.

4. "Gettysburg." Directed by Ron Maxwell. Tristar Television, 1993.

5. Taylor, Howard, and Mrs. Howard Taylor. *The Growth of a Work of God* (Ch. 19). 1875. In "Catalogue of Books," *World Invisible.*

http://www.worldinvisible.com/library/hudsontaylor/hudsontaylorv2/hudsontaylorv219.htm.

6. Rogers, Bruce A., and John P. Schutt. "December 10." *A Season of Advent Devotions.* Long Neck United Methodist Church, 2016. http://www.longneck-umc.com/hp_wordpress/wp-content/uploads/2016/11/advent_2016.pdf.

7. Brooks, Phillips. Quoted in *The Westminster Collection of Christian Quotations*, edited by Martin H. Manser (Westminster John Knox Press, 2001), 23.

About the Author

Tom and Kathy Kinnan have been married forty-five years and have two married children and six grandchildren. Prior to retiring, Kathy taught humanities at Whitefield Academy, a Christian classical school, and she puts up with a weird and wacky husband.

With forty-one years of pastoring and forty-five years of ministry, Tom brings a depth of knowledge as well as tenderness and compassion to his subject matter. Known for insight, humor, and challenging teaching, his presentations are anointed of God. Tom has traveled internationally as a speaker at colleges, churches, conventions, retreats, and camps. He has extensive experience serving missionaries and in mission fields.

Tom's heart is to see people in the church become equipped to live their lives fully devoted to Christ in the community where God plants them to be a light. He does not want to maintain a church, but wants the church to be a living and growing body of believers.

Tom is the founder and president of Good Shepherd Ministries and serves with New Church Specialties as an interim pastor.

About Sermon To Book

SermonToBook.com began with a simple belief: that sermons should be touching lives, *not* collecting dust. That's why we turn sermons into high-quality books that are accessible to people all over the globe.

Turning your sermon series into a book exposes more people to God's Word, better equips you for counseling, accelerates future sermon prep, adds credibility to your ministry, and even helps make ends meet during tight times.

John 21:25 tells us that the world itself couldn't contain the books that would be written about the work of Jesus Christ. Our mission is to try anyway. Because in heaven, there will no longer be a need for sermons or books. Our time is now.

If God so leads you, we'd love to work with you on your sermon or sermon series.

Visit www.sermontobook.com to learn more.

Made in the USA
San Bernardino, CA
24 October 2018